A
PATTERN
GARDEN

THE 14 ESSENTIAL GARDEN PATTERNS

1. SCALE

2. GARDEN ROOMS

3. PATHWAYS

4. BRIDGES

5. GATES

6. SHELTERS

7. BORDERS

8. PATIOS

9. SHEDS

10. FOCAL POINTS

11. WATER

12. ORNAMENTATION

13. CONTAINERS

14. MATERIALS

A PATTERN GARDEN

THE ESSENTIAL

ELEMENTS OF GARDEN

MAKING

VALERIE EASTON

PHOTOGRAPHY BY

JACQUELINE KOCH

WITH RICHARD HARTLAGE AND ALLAN MANDELL

FOREWORD BY

SUZY BALES

TIMBER PRESS

Published in 2007 by
Timber Press, Inc.
The Haseltine Building
133 S.W. Second Avenue, Suite 450
Portland, Oregon 97204-3527, U.S.A.
www.timberpress.com
For contact information regarding editorial, marketing, sales, and
distribution in the United Kingdom, see www.timberpress.co.uk.

ISBN 978-0-88192-780-1

Page 2: A grand water feature matches the scale and tone of this highly-designed Connecticut garden, with fieldstone collected from the property and fountainheads carved from bluestone. *Pages 4-5:* A floating cedar deck, casual fluffs of ornamental grass, and the ease of a weathered Adirondack chair soften the transition between house and beach. *Page 6:* Fiery flower stalks of Crocosmia 'Lucifer' are shown off against a pale yellow fence, where their distinctive shape and hot color have great impact. *Page 10:* Gates are one of the most satisfying of garden patterns, serving as portal and making an occasion out of entry and exit.

Book design: Karen Schober
Copy editor: Alice Copp Smith
Produced by Unleashed Book Development

All photographs are by Jacqueline Koch, with the following exceptions:
Copyright © Richard Hartlage: pages 2, 26, 28, 32, 33 bottom, 39, 41, 47, 48, 55, 59, 60, 63 top, 63 box, 64, 71, 73, 83 top, 89, 90, 102 top, 102 bottom, 110, 111, 114, 118, 127, 131, 135 bottom, 146, 158, 162, 167, and 175.
Copyright © Allan Mandell: pages 25, 27, 30, 43, 45, 46 top, 56, 62, 65 top, 75, 77, 78, 80, 81, 82 bottom, 91, 92, 97, 99, 103, 117, 130, 133, 152, 159, 161 bottom-left, 164, 174, and 181.

Grasscrete, Plexiglas, Sunbrella, and Trex are registered trademarks.

Printed in China

Catalog records for this book are available from the Library of Congress and the British Library.

DEDICATION

TO GREG, KATIE, SPENCER, AND COOPER,

WITH LOVE AND APPRECIATION FOR YOUR SUPPORT, PATIENCE, AND

FOND COMPANIONSHIP, IN AND OUT OF THE GARDEN.

CONTENTS

FOREWORD BY SUZY BALES

CREATING A GARDEN IS LIKE FALLING IN LOVE: The heart rules the head, and the best decisions are emotional, not intellectual. In my experience, emotion is the secret ingredient of every good garden.

We all have the ability to open our eyes and follow our hearts, and in *A Pattern Garden,* Valerie Easton tells us how to tap into that emotion. This book opens the door between the past and the present, altering and refining the way we see gardens. "The most successful and satisfying gardens are designed by owners themselves, or with their close participation," says Valerie. She encourages gardeners to embrace what is special about their gardens. She inspires everyone to be better than they thought they could be—more creative, more daring, more heart strong than headstrong. If you don't love a plant, it won't thrive in your garden!

One February, a few years back, I visited Valerie's own garden. Even in the mild climate of Seattle, February is not a month for garden visits. Yet, there was much to see

and learn from her terraced, quarter-acre slope. Every nook and cranny was planted to produce year-round flowers and foliage. Paths, stairs, and arbors crisscrossed, uniting three different levels. Because it rains so much in Seattle, she designed walks of clean, hard surfaces extending from every door out into the garden. She didn't hesitate to mix shrubs, trees, vegetables, herbs, and perennials. Containers softened the hard surfaces.

Entering the property from the bottom of the hill and winding my way up took time. There was so much to stop and see along the way. Tucked into the top terrace, hidden from view, was a small patio, snugly fitted with two Adirondack chairs among potted flowers, looking out over the borrowed scenery of an uninterrupted view of Lake Washington. Good gardens such as this come in all shapes and sizes and are planted on all different terrains.

Clearly, Valerie knows her stuff! In *A Pattern Garden,* she shares first-hand experiences and articulates complex concepts, simply and gracefully. She waded through the classic *A Pattern Language*, an 1,100-page architectural tome that includes 250 garden patterns, to thoughtfully interpret 14 key patterns suited for home gardeners today. The precise yet flexible patterns help demystify garden design and thinking in three dimensions. They convey how people move through space, as well as touch on spirituality, or how space makes you feel. They firmly unite the house with the garden.

The choice of patterns and plants brings out the individuality and personality of the gardener. The fun begins once these initial decisions have been made and implemented. Like all living things, a garden has a mind of its own, and plants do talk back. There is no such thing as a green or black thumb; either you love plants or you don't and, believe me, the plants know. The plants adopt a loving gardener—nurturing, comforting, and feeding you, generously giving back happiness and satisfaction. A garden in the course of a year can be colorful, calm, messy, orderly, dehydrated or water logged, and so heart-stoppingly beautiful, it takes your breath away. The joy that radiates from the bloom of a flower can't be overstated. A garden that is loved and cherished is always even more glorious than expected.

And if there are problems, there is no need to worry. *A Pattern Garden* introduces *wabi sabi,* the art of nature's unadorned truths. So, you'll never again have to say, "You should have been here last week."

"Blemishes and irregularities are good things that bestow character and ensure modesty," Valerie says.

After finishing the book, I took a new look at my own garden, seeing it as it ought to be, rather than as it is. I saw many new possibilities. Valerie startled me into paying attention. Among the many eye-opening revelations: "Fill narrow borders with *huge* plants to create an Alice-down-the-rabbit-hole effect of shrinking the viewer. A single large object tricks a small space into seeming larger." "Cast a spell with the placement of a door, add mystery and suspense by planting a hedge." "Put a lid on the garden" with an arbor. "Make the trip to the front door worthwhile." Although I don't personally anticipate erecting a pyramid of bowling balls anytime soon, I like knowing it is a possibility. The patterns I learned about from Valerie prompted me to make changes in my own garden.

It's safe to say that this is the only book on garden design you'll need. It holds the tools to design a personal and fulfilling outdoor space. I predict *A Pattern Garden* will become a classic. It will give new gardeners the confidence they need to get started, help experienced gardeners reflect on the essentials of good garden design, and inspire us all to follow our hearts.

SUZY BALES is Senior Editor for Gardening and Outdoor Living at Better Homes & Gardens, and a former New York Times garden columnist. She is the author of 12 books, most recently *Suzy Bales' Down-to-Earth Gardener.*

ACKNOWLEDGMENTS

≁

I MOST WANT TO THANK ALL THE PEOPLE who have opened their gardens to me and shared their stories. Gardeners are generous with their passions, preferences, triumphs, and disappointments, as well as advice, plants, and weather lore. I've learned so much from all of you, and your creativity, hope, and perseverance have inspired me.

I also want to thank my editors and collaborators at *Pacific Northwest,* the *Seattle Times* Sunday magazine, for their belief in me and for setting high standards. There's no better way to learn how to write than to turn in a column every week, year after year. I appreciate that you've published, edited, and coached me, while encouraging me to search out the best garden stories for more than a decade.

And, of course, thanks to Christopher Alexander and his co-authors of *A Pattern Language,* the book that has so influenced my ideas about scale, space, and design over the years.

Readers can see for themselves why I'm so grateful to photographers Jacqueline Koch, Allan Mandell, and Richard Hartlage. It's a treat and an education to see gardens through your eyes and your lenses.

I wouldn't be a garden writer without the support of my gardening friends. Heartfelt thanks to Suzy Bales for your insightful foreword and to Robyn Atkinson, Dan Hinkley, David Lewis, George Little, Richard Hartlage, Stacie Crooks, David Laskin, Sue Nicol, Ray Larson, Alice Doyle, and my sister Joan Works for obsessing about plants and gardens with me over the years. Thanks for knowing more than I do and always being willing to help me out.

The look of this book, its organization, and even the fact that it exists is due to the commitment, hard work, and talent of Kate Rogers and Karen Schober, editor and designer respectively. You're both a joy to work with. Thanks to copy editor Alice Copp Smith, who saved me from many a grammatical embarrassment, and to Tom Fischer and Timber Press for believing in this book throughout its lengthy genesis.

Design elements create a transition from forest to outdoor sitting room, with an arbor for shelter and scale and a twig rocker for comfort and repose.

INTRODUCTION:

WHY USE PATTERNS IN THE GARDEN?

BECAUSE I AM A GARDEN COLUMNIST, it is critical that I design and tend my own garden, for what I learn out there in the dirt informs all my writing. I found the courage to create a garden in large part from what I learned years ago in Christopher Alexander's book *A Pattern Language* (Oxford University Press, 1977), a groundbreaking slab of a book that advocates the idea that people should design for themselves their houses, gardens, streets, and communities.

The rhythm of alternating pavers and grass offer a study in soft and hard, living and non-living. They draw the eye, and the feet, toward the mysterious gap between crisply pruned hedges.

The surprising revelation that Alexander introduced was not only that they should design, but that they *could*. For many years I've also been visiting and writing about other people's gardens, and I've learned that the most successful and satisfying gardens are designed by the owners themselves, or with their close participation. This makes sense to me, for I believe that the garden calls up our deepest instincts, and it is from these instincts that good design is born. These archetypal ideas and longings are what *A Pattern Language* is all about.

Despite its length (more than 1,100 pages!), dense writing, and blurry black-and-white photos, Alexander's book has for decades influenced my thinking, and that of a great many other people, about how we live and move through spaces, how and why we respond to our environment. I remember as I read the book experiencing a great number of moments when I closed my eyes and sank into remembering the felt experience of different houses and gardens. It explains so much about what makes a home warm and inviting, why some gardens enchant and others merely impress. We know how we feel when entering a space; *A Pattern Language* puts these human instincts into words, breaks them into "patterns" replicable by those of us not trained in the design professions. Thinking of design in terms of such basic patterns helps us to understand why we feel comfortable in a space.

Following along a curved path or wall reflects a pattern with universal appeal. Hostas and ferns soften the edges, while low hedging mirrors the shape and curve of the wall.

That book came about when a group of architects and architecture students at the University of California at Berkeley worked together to articulate their design ideas and experiences, distilling them down to some 250 patterns that affect the way we live. These professionals were able to translate "designer brain" for those of us not endowed with the ability to think in three dimensions. Although the book included little about residential garden design outside of trees and vegetable gardens, most of its ideas translate beautifully to gardens because they deal with the underlying patterns of behavior and form that shape our collective experience and stir the emotions.

Even today, the configurations that appeal to our deepest instincts help me to understand why some gardens succeed while others are only showpieces. Many of the gardens I visit coax you through the front gate, draw you in, surprise, delight, and invite you to lounge on an outdoor chaise for a nap or pause beneath a shady arbor. Others, though visually impressive, provoke nothing more than visual admiration. Perhaps it is the difference between simply looking at a garden and feeling yourself moving through the garden, experiencing it on a level that engages far more than your eyes and your intellect. Henry Beston said, "A garden is a mirror of the mind," but this is true only in gardens that go beyond design conventions to truly reflect the passions and interests of their inhabitants. With my own book, *A Pattern Garden,* I hope to inspire gardeners to create spaces that are more than simply outdoor living rooms or collections of plants. The archetypal patterns of garden-making, based on proportions and what our own senses tell us, can be used to make satisfying and memorable gardens. These patterns give a coherence to garden design; they allow us to communicate our creativity and aesthetics, for they are deeply rooted in the nature of things. Perhaps delving deep to understand these patterns is a little bit like outdoor feng shui for Westerners. It's a way to capture our "felt sense" of a garden and transform that felt sense into replicable concepts, or patterns.

Green shades in an espaliered apple tree, clipped boxwood, leaves of mayapple, and a foam of lady's mantle offer a display of contrasting textures and shapes.

The garden patterns in this book have been chosen and named because they are quintessential for good garden-making. We instinctively look for and treasure certain specific elements, and working with these elements is the basis for all good garden design. Just as we naturally love to curl up in a cushioned window seat or draw a chair to a warm fireside, so do we enjoy passing beneath the dappled shade of a vine-draped pergola. Certain garden elements offer universal appeal: garden gates, white arbors covered in pink roses, mossy stones, private courtyards, curving pathways, a pair of Adirondack chairs, still ponds, covered porches—we seek such elements in every garden we enter, and relax when we find them. Because each such element, or pattern, is archetypal, site is transcended, and any pattern can be easily adapted and made your own whether you live on a steep hillside, beside a bay, on a flat suburban

A soft, puffy armchair of moss is both focal point and art object in this Asian-inspired courtyard garden.

lot, or in the woods. It isn't sun, shade, or topography that matters, but rather whether there are parts of the garden you long to spend time in, places where the sun falls across your face in winter, areas with views or cozy intimacy. These patterns transcend not only site but style; they can be adapted to English-, Asian-, or Mediterranean-style gardens. A little bridge crossing a dry gully can be a simple slab of stone, or it can be arched and decorated with Japanese scrollwork. It is the crossing over that matters, not the materials—the feeling of leaving behind one part of the garden and arriving somewhere new.

Alexander's landmark book points out that such design elements as open hearths, alcoves, bay windows, verandas, and fireside corners are some of the components that make a house comfortable and desirable. To pattern a garden is a little more difficult, for gardens are more dynamic than bricks and mortar. The fact that gardens are inherently a metaphor for change is a large part of their appeal. But such constant flux can be a challenge. Our experience of gardens is dramatically influenced by wind, rain, and sun, by deer and slugs, by plants as they spread, mature, and die. Think how you feel in a garden on a mild spring afternoon when the bulbs are bursting through the ground and the trees freshly coated in green. Then picture that same garden during a November windstorm when leaves crunch underfoot and swirl overhead, or on a winter morning when the skeletons of perennials sparkle with frost. But despite the mutability of gardens, the essential patterns, the proportions, the sense of arrival, feelings of shelter and refuge, enclosure and exposure, the canopy and the paths underfoot all remain to form the archetypal garden that stirs our hearts and invites us in.

This book attempts to put into language and capture in photographs the underlying patterns of good garden design, to connect our thoughts with our feelings, thus making it possible to create satisfying and rewarding gardens. Understanding what it is we love about gardens enables us to build the essence of a garden that we intuitively feel is right for us. The first chapter introduces the essential patterns. Subsequent chapters explore each of the pattern elements, showing them in a wide variety of garden styles, geographical locations, and sites. Taken alone, paired, or in combinations, the patterns create a coherent experience that excites, stirs the senses, and satisfies our notions of what a garden can be.

You'll see that these patterns are in part all about intangible—how we move through space; where we feel protected and where we feel exposed; how we pass through sunlight and shade; the relationship of indoors and out. The book explores how these seeming intangibles can in fact be carefully choreographed to create the experience you seek in your own garden.

*A simple composition of ribbon grass (*Phalaris arundinacea*) and an unplanted pot is an artful composition of contrasts: rough and smooth, bulky and slim, dark and light. (Warning: ribbon grass can be invasive.)*
NEXT PAGE: *The architecture of the house is extended out on this large property to inject structure into a rambling, plant-rich landscape.*

chapter one

CONTEXT

THE ESSENCE OF THE GARDEN:

CONTEXT, CHANGE, AND PATTERN-MAKING

GARDENS HAVE BEEN USED throughout literature as a metaphor for life, and no wonder, for the essence of a garden is change. At the heart of the garden, beyond concepts like landscape, plantings, and site planning, lies a state of constant flux. When we think of our gardens, we envision their beauty, the toil and frustrations, our joys and defeats, the passing of the seasons. But our deepest satisfactions are found in the profound changes we admire, bemoan, and participate in right outside our own back doors. Change is the teacher, the dynamic, and the moving force in garden-making.

If life on earth is as mutable as the physicists now tell us, perhaps it is only through gardening that we are able to grasp the underlying nature of this perpetual flow and interconnectedness. Maybe the key to quantum physics lies in planting a perennial garden. An intimate involvement with a garden over days, seasons, and years allows us to experience and digest what Carl Jung called "the terrible ambiguity of immediate experience." Much of this ambiguity lies in our relationship with change, so relentlessly encapsulated in the experience of making and tending a garden.

The Japanese are masters at expressing garden as metaphor, with bridges, reflections, stone, and water as iconic elements repeated in pleasing patterns.

This garden offers a variety of destinations: The distant, vine-draped doorway beckons intriguingly, while stairs and pathways are partly obscured by groupings of tall summer flowers.

Garden change is multilayered—it seeps into our bones, brains, and subconscious because we experience it in minutes, hours, and years. We know that our lives can change in the instant of a baby's birth, a car crash, a sudden death. How to live with that? As we work in a garden through the seasons, we come to understand and accept change as the very essence and rhythm of the garden. We experience buds opening, petals scattering, leaves falling. A single cloud passing over the sun dims and softens colors, and a chill descends in perception if not in temperature. When the sun pops out again, colors shimmer and intensify in response, textures are highlighted as if picked out by individual rays of light. Or, in some climates and on some days, the garden seems to bleach out as pale as old bones beneath the strength of the sun.

Snow is nature's magician, for it homogenizes all of outdoors in a supreme transformation of light, color, and texture. When you wake up on a snowy morning, even

before you open your eyes, the quality of the light on your closed lids will tell you that the earth outside your windows is monotone. But even transitory touches of frost, wind, drizzle, or rain, or a shroud of fog, all transform how the garden looks and how we feel when we're in it. Temperature and weather affect both plants and people, for flowers open to the sun, plants wilt down in the heat, quiver in the rain, toss and bend in the wind—reactions not unlike our own. Plants derive their life force from the sun, the soil, and the rain—and, much as we forget it, so do we.

A single day in the garden includes the drama of new life, ripening, seed dispersal, decline, and death. Daylilies are so called because they open each bud only once and for

THE CONCEPT OF *WABI SABI*

Wabi sabi is an ancient Japanese art that celebrates impermanence, revels in the transitory, and elevates the humble to such an extent you can't help but think its originators had a garden in mind. This is an aesthetic that finds sweetness in melancholy, simplicity, and restraint. The concept is so Zenlike, so shrouded in centuries of interpretation and mystery, as to be nearly indefinable. Here's what is so endearing—in *wabi sabi*, blemishes and irregularities are good things that bestow character and ensure modesty. The tea ceremony, Japanese garden design, haiku, and flower arranging have all been inspired by *wabi sabi*. It's also what has kept them subtle and intimate arts.

A love of the unconventional is a big part of *wabi sabi*, and it's especially relevant to garden design. The Zen monks had quite a radical worldview, not for the sake of being unconventional, but because they believed different viewpoints stimulated different ways of perceiving art. How freeing is that? Where better than the garden to experiment, mess about, and personalize while testing perceptions? *Wabi sabi* prizes mystery and intrigue; when you step outside your back door into the garden, you're submerged in the ambiguity offered up by nature every day of the year. How comforting to relax into it rather than try to control it. Other *wabi sabi* principles, such as attention to detail and a desire for simplicity and balance, serve the garden designer well.

This tradition also addresses the current buzz of sustainability. There's a Japanese expression saying that someone who makes poor-quality things is worse than a thief because these things don't last or provide true satisfaction. Durable elements that last in nature as well as in the heart of the gardener won't need replacing for a very long time.

The spirit of *wabi sabi* lies in nature's unadorned truths, something we touch every time we dig in the soil, harvest a tomato, or turn the mulch pile. Gardeners are realists, made that way through participating in nature's rhythms, watching the ebb and flow of the life force in the plants we tend. We think of this as science; *wabi sabi* reminds us that it is art.

the space of a single day. Flowers close and open with the light, releasing their perfume to tempt bees and bugs. Some, like the brugmansias, wait until nightfall to release their sweet scent in hopes of attracting night-flying moths in to pollinate their flowers. The garden changes in vitality and perception from the pearly light of morning to the direct light of midday, and again in the brilliance or duskiness of the evening sky.

Over the course of the year, garden change obviously takes on a seasonal rhythm. How many Japanese haiku have been composed in the attempt to suggest, in three concise lines, the essence of seasonal change? These brief poems evoke the emotion wrought by the silky pink of cherry petals, a shroud of fog, the blaze of autumn leaves. Just think of each plant, from the tallest tree to a ground-hugging perennial, cycling through its emergence, bloom, fruiting, and decline. Then magnify this effect over an entire garden of plants, and you get the idea of how seasonal glory bursts from the garden. At the cusp of each season, when such change is at its most intense, a garden overwhelms with its flowery ardor or bleakness of bare branches. And beneath it all is the beat of time and change: if leaves are turning color today, surely the branches will soon be bare. Our emotions are closely tied to the burgeoning optimism of springtime, the relaxing warmth of summer, the gentle melancholy of autumn, the chill austerity of winter. But there is great comfort in the cyclical nature of this change. As the days darken and shorten, we celebrate the renewal of spring by pushing aside fallen leaves to dig into the still-warm soil and plant bulbs. In the quiet cold of winter, we'll go outside and look for the tips of those bulbs to push up fresh green through the near-frozen soil.

Then there's macro-change, over the years and over the decades. With time, a garden grows large, dense, and

Perennial gardens celebrate seasonal change, while aged brick, stucco walls, and evergreen plantings evoke a garden's timelessness.

shadowy. Or perhaps wind or ice storms cull the trees and open it up again. Tree trunks gnarl, vines grow thick and twisted, stones sprout a soft pelt of moss, and lichen drips from tree branches. Even the man-made parts of the garden change: structures weather and sag, roofs grow mossy, stone walls crumble. This impermanence is celebrated in the Japanese concept of *wabi sabi*, which appreciates mellowing, decay, and imperfection. *Wabi sabi* recognizes the beauty that exists in the transition between the coming and going of life, a situation on perpetual display in the garden.

And yet … gardens last. We find them so nurturing and reassuring because, despite their being in a state of constant flux, they persist through the years and decades. In parts of the world older than our own, gardens have stood for centuries, and while maintained or planted differently over the years, retain their ancient stone grottoes, pools, pathways. And this is where the human influence plays such a vital part, because it is the patterns we impose that are the most permanent part of gardens. We layer our patterns of shaping, structures, and designed plantings in harmony or juxtaposition with nature's inexorable rhythms.

We might find these patterns consoling, disturbing, comfortable, beautiful, exciting—it doesn't matter. Gardens are all of these things. The point is to choose our patterns consciously, to take joy in their making, as well as in the changes that will surely come, in the next minute and over the years. We can choose the patterns that best suit our site, our aesthetics, and our emotions only by understanding which patterns we enjoy, which are meaningful, and which make the garden satisfying for us. Westerners have striven to understand and translate the art of feng shui for centuries, but at its core I think it addresses just this issue. Feng shui helps us to understand why it is we feel comfortable or not in a space. Only by figuring out what it is we like or dislike about what we see, feel, or experience can we then duplicate it, manipulating the patterns we like best to fit our specific space, situation, and aspect. Perhaps it is no coincidence, with the ideas of feng shui and *wabi sabi* to draw upon, that Asian garden patterns, more than any other garden tradition, capture the timelessness of gardens. By suggesting permanence with stone, evergreens, and water, Asian gardens highlight the brevity of a single camellia blossom or the flare of autumn color set against an unchanging green backdrop.

The fourteen essential patterns laid out in this book are elements you can fuse into any style of garden to make it more comfortably your own. First, we'll consider the attributes and drawbacks of your unique garden site. Once you're firmly grounded in your own garden reality, it's time to consider the specific patterns. Scale is the all-important first pattern that creates ease and comfort. If you get your garden scale right, everything else will fit into place.

With the second pattern, that of Garden Rooms, you begin to shape space, to consider use and purpose. The third pattern, Pathways, leads us to consider both the how and why of moving through gardens. Bridges and Gates,

patterns four and five, also facilitate moving about the garden, each with its own potential to reveal, disclose, and decorate.

Patterns six and seven are Shelters and Borders, which involve drawing lines, shaping space, and casting shade. Pattern eight, Focal Points, is integral to all good garden design, as important to the eye as to the camera. Patterns nine and ten are Sheds and Work Spaces, and Patios and Terraces—all of these elements being vital to living and working in a garden. Pattern eleven is all about Water, whether in a stream, a waterfall, or a simple birdbath.

The art of gardening comes into play with patterns twelve and thirteen, Ornamentation and Containers. The fourteenth and last pattern, Materials, underlies all the rest, for we shape the garden underfoot, overhead, and all around us by our choice of wood, paving, gravel, recycled materials, or brand-new elements. These are the fourteen vital garden patterns, both concepts and tools, that we can use to shape a garden that pleases and endures.

All too often we start designing our gardens by thinking—and then fretting—about where the garbage cans should go, whether the material of the driveway suits the house, and which tree to plant where. We obsess over all the shades of delphinium blue, or which pulmonaria leaves are spotted in the brightest silver. Perhaps it's true that God is in the details. But to end up with a garden that is greater than the sum of its parts, you must be sure to look up from the details during the course of your garden-making. Gardening is about nothing less than the life force and the endless mutability of nature. If you keep this realization firmly in mind as you create and tend your garden, it can't fail to be satisfying on every level from the mundane to the profound.

LEFT: *The yin and yang of change and permanence is captured in this tableau of a heavy wooden bench set upon stone and backed by an airy Japanese maple.*
RIGHT: *Mixed border plantings are in constant flux through the seasons, magnifying the beat of time at the heart of all our garden endeavors.*

FAR LEFT: *Autumn's glory is a reminder of the bare branches and dark days to come, so don't be in too much of a hurry to rake up the leaves. The tree is a yoshino cherry (*Prunus x yedoensis*); the dog is Maggie, a wheaten terrier.*

LEFT: Canna pretoria, *also known as Bengal Tiger, is a Las Vegas showgirl of a plant, with bold leaves and orange flowers that radiate the overblown nature of high summer.*

BELOW: *Spring is a softer season, with the promise of heat and summer to come. Allium buds develop tantalizingly slowly, with the pale blue flower spikes of camassia carrying the show until their flowers open later in May.*

NEXT PAGE: *The success of every garden pattern depends on taking advantage of your unique site; here, a stone terrace overlooks a teahouse and pond in the foreground with a distant territorial view stretching out beyond.*

chapter two

SITE

YOUR UNIQUE SITE:

WEATHER, SOIL, TOPOGRAPHY, AND VIEWS

THE BASIS OF ANY SUCCESSFUL GARDEN PATTERN is to garden where you live. This may sound obvious, but all too often we ignore the realities of our yards in pursuit of the garden in our imaginations. But plants grow in the ground, subject to all the vagaries of climate, and it's only when we thoroughly understand the properties of our own regions that we can use that knowledge to push at the boundaries of what is possible. Every garden pattern

*The quieter beauties of winter are captured in an inspired combination of silvery artemisia and bristly purple fountain grass (*Pennisetum setaceum *'Rubrum').*

depends on understanding your own unique site and making the most of its soil, weather, views, light, and topography.

I've known so many people who have moved to a new area of the country, eager to start gardening in a fresh place, only to re-create the gardens from their previous homes. Or worse yet, to create a Moroccan courtyard or a canna-banana extravaganza totally unrelated to where they live. Playing with microclimates and indulging in garden fantasies are part of the fascination of gardening, but they work only when firmly rooted in the reality of your own garden's ecology. Our gardens ground us in our natural environment, and give us a sense of place—but only if we understand and acknowledge what that place really offers us as gardeners.

Gardening is a weather-dependent activity, so this topic has taken on a new urgency in recent years as our long-established and expected weather patterns change precipitously. Winters have been warmer and wetter, or colder and drier, and summers often hotter than usual, all around the country and the world. It's hard to even know what is usual anymore when it comes to weather. Plants bloom earlier than anticipated, live through warm winters, or are toppled by high winds. Droughts and storms seem more virulent and frequent. Meteorologists are cautious, advising that it takes as long as thirty years to distinguish a climate trend. Gardeners scramble to adjust their long-held beliefs about their climate and what they can grow. Faced with such global climate uncertainty, we need to observe the garden carefully and be more flexible than in the past. Although we don't have to banish all that weather knowledge we've accumulated over the years, we at least need to be willing to adjust our thinking and beliefs, season by season, to the new realities of weather flux.

TEMPERATURE

The hard, cold truths of gardening reality are often colder than we care to admit, despite global warming. What you can grow successfully depends most of all on the low temperatures in your area. Even freeze damage isn't an absolute, but depends on timing: a sharp freeze in November may kill off a slew of borderline plants, while several days of the same temperatures in January, once plants have hardened off, cause much less devastation.

There are many mitigating factors that may help your garden get through the winter intact. Well-drained soil helps, for often plants die of rot in soggy winter soils where otherwise they might survive a freeze. Do you reliably have snow, which is a great insulator, during the cold-

est months of winter? How about temperature mitigation from nearby bodies of water? A nearby lake or bay can warm up a garden by as much as ten degrees, taking the edge off winter cold. Where does the fog lie and the frost collect on cold mornings? It pays to study all these things about your garden, trying to toss out preconceived notions of what zone you live in, until you truly understand the microclimates in your own garden. It's fine to use the USDA climate zone map, based on extremes of cold, as a starting point, but I've often heard people exclaim, "I'm a zone 6—I couldn't possibly grow that," as if a zone number was stamped on their forehead. Zones aren't absolutes, but a useful concept. Also, you can thwart the cold and protect your garden by mulching, by wrapping more tender plants in bubble wrap or even bath towels on the coldest nights, or by bringing plants in to overwinter in a garage, garden shed, or greenhouse.

Then there's heat to consider. The American Horticultural Society has recently produced a plant heat zone map (page 40), in contrast to the more familiar USDA climate zone map based on cold temperatures. Plants suffer from high temperatures and humidity just as people do, but their wilting can be permanent. In other areas, despite sunny days, it never really gets hot enough to ripen tomatoes or bring semitropical plants into bloom. The AHS Plant Heat Zone Map clarifies the importance heat as well as cold plays in creating a successful garden.

And then there is the concept of microclimates, which are created by the lay of the land or can be influenced by placement of fences, houses, and paving. You can clue in to your own garden's microclimates by paying attention to where the wind whistles through, frost collects, or heat gathers and reflects to create warm pockets for ripening figs or bringing tropicals into early bloom. You can mitigate or exploit the microclimates in your garden, but first you need to notice and understand them to take full advantage of what they offer in terms of comfort, and possibilities for plants.

And garden temperatures, or microclimates, aren't just about plants, but also affect the architecture of your garden. In cooler zones, where the temperature reaches above

The casual, even scruffy look of native desert plants complement the strong, solid bulk of stucco garden walls that appear as if built from the earth itself.

80°F only for a few days or a few weeks of the year, you'll want to build a patio on the south or west side of your house, and perhaps invest in an overhead heat lamp if you like to eat dinner outside in the summer. In California or the Southwest, a deck or patio will get the most use if it's located on the north side of the house, or beneath a tree or an arbor to cast afternoon shade. If you live high on a

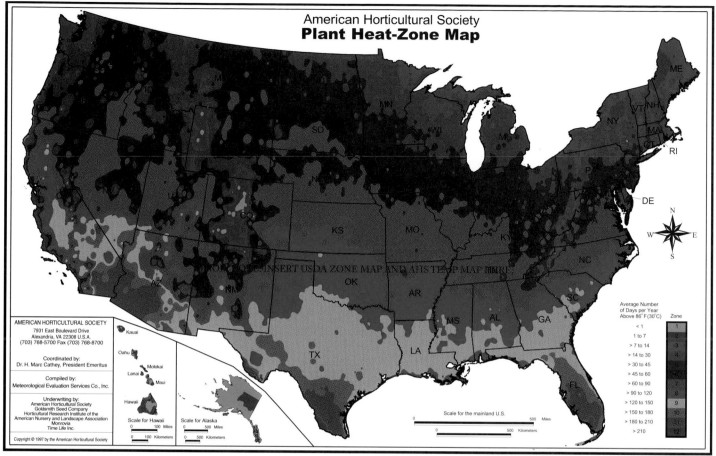

American Horticultural Society
Plant Heat-Zone Map

AMERICAN HORTICULTURAL SOCIETY
7931 East Boulevard Drive
Alexandria, VA 22308 U.S.A.
(703) 768-5700 Fax (703) 768-8700

Coordinated by:
Dr. H. Marc Cathey, President Emeritus

Compiled by:
Meteorological Evaluation Services Co., Inc.

Underwriting by:
American Horticultural Society
Goldsmith Seed Company
Horticultural Research Institute of the
American Nursery and Landscape Association
Monrovia
Time Life Inc.

Copyright © 1997 by the American Horticultural Society

Average Number
of Days per Year
Above 86° F (30°C)   Zone

< 1	1
1 to 7	2
> 7 to 14	3
> 14 to 30	4
> 30 to 45	5
> 45 to 60	6
> 60 to 90	7
> 90 to 120	8
> 120 to 150	9
> 150 to 180	10
> 180 to 210	11
> 210	12

Reproduced with permission of the American Horticultural Society (www.ahs.org).

windy hillside, or near the sea, windbreaks are as important for people as plants, for both need shelter from the gusts. So consider how the sun slants, where the wind blows, how the house or trees cast shadows, as you plan your outdoor living areas as well as your plant placement.

SOIL, SUN, AND TOPOGRAPHY

The dirt that lies beneath your feet may well be the factor that most limits your choice of garden patterns. We can improve soil to a great degree, drain it, double-dig it, build raised beds, but the soil, slopes, sun, and shade of your property are its essence and can only be tinkered with so much.

You can get help from local extension agents and master gardeners (connected with the land grant university closest to you) who are knowledgeable about the soils in your region and about soil test kits. But quite often soil varies greatly in composition and acidity in different spots throughout a single property. In addition, its drainage potential is greatly affected by the slant of the land. Toward the top of slopes the soil is usually drier; slopes typically drain much better than flats; and the area near the bottom of a slope is often mucky and wet. So observe, pay attention to drainage, watch which plants flourish and which decline. Then you can set right out to improve the soil.

No matter what your soil is like, regular mulching and adding plenty of compost will help, for organic matter

*Every season has its iconic plants, and the blast of staghorn sumac's (*Rhus typhina*) colorful foliage and fuzzy red cones transforms this rockery into a display of October brilliance.*

lightens up heavy soil and enriches sandy soil. Any organic gardening book will give you all the basics on making good dirt. Beyond that, growing healthy plants depends on careful observation, and matching plants to the places where they'll do best. Instead of trying to "improve" a boggy, low-lying area of the garden, cele-

LEFT: *The more you're able to incorporate archetypal patterns into your garden, the less it's simply an outdoor living room or collection of plants.*
BELOW: *A mossy wooden bench sets the tone for the simplicity of this naturalistic garden, as well as providing a destination.*

brate it by planting giant-leafed gunneras, rodgersias, and ligularias, which will grow large and luscious with wet feet. And you'll reduce your water bill by gardening with nature rather than in opposition to it. Woodland plants such as epimedium (*Epimedium* spp.) and male ferns (*Dryopteris filix-mas*) take to difficult dry shade, and all the Mediterranean silverlings, such as lavender and sages, enjoy hot, exposed hillsides. There are so many tempting plants to try, no matter where you garden, that even when you limit yourself to what will thrive in your existing garden conditions, you'll have plenty to choose from.

And what about cases of absurdly poor soil, deep, dank shade, or extreme exposure? Or what if you simply lust for plants unable to survive the realities of what your garden or climate has to offer? The solution lies in raised beds, pots, greenhouses, cold frames, or even unheated garages. In raised beds, it's possible to provide near-perfect soil conditions. You can move pots about into sun or shade, as well as control the soil conditions in each to suit what you want to plant. And you can cosset tender plants over the winter in a greenhouse, or cut them back and drag them into a garage or shed.

ASPECT AND VIEWS

Whether you live on a tiny city lot with close-by neighbors, atop a remote hillside with views out to water and mountains, or on a spacious suburban acre, you are faced with the choice of developing enclosure or living with openness. Do you want your garden to relate more to the house, or to the natural or man-made surroundings? How to take advantage of views yet provide privacy? Do you love morning light or late afternoon warmth, or do you prefer to shade out the sun's rays?

The traditional American suburban model is of a fenced back garden and a front lawn open to the neighborhood, but there are a great many more possibilities.

Patterns of courtyards, hedging, or artificial screening, and strategically placed trees all create privacy. The Japanese art of "borrowed scenery" enhances a distant view. A panoramic view is a more difficult prospect. A gardener can choose to compete with the view by creating garden pyrotechnics in the foreground. This approach can lead to a Disneyland of a garden that busily vies for attention with the view, bringing out the best in neither. Or you can choose to use the garden to make the most of the view by creating a quiet space that leads the eye to the majesty beyond. Some gardeners decide to avoid all reference to the greater landscape and to create a garden quite distinct and separate from the natural surroundings. So much of how it feels to be in a garden, as well as what will grow well, depends upon light, view, shade, and shadows, and these can be manipulated to create warmth, coolness, brightness, darkness, mood, varying growing conditions, and a view out or a sense of secure enclosure.

In the next chapters you'll find garden patterns that deal with weather, topography, and site in clever and lovely ways. Some gardeners choose to reinforce the ecology of their site by using mostly native plants to create lower-maintenance, green nature sanctuaries. Others intersperse native plants, to attract birds and wildlife, with showier ornamental plantings. The Zen of Japanese gardens, with water, stones, and a minimum of plants, suits some environments and gardeners beautifully, while others plant a sturdy backbone of hardy plants and then push the boundaries of their climate zones in surprising displays of horticultural bravado. In every case, successful gardens are based on a thorough knowledge of local conditions, and on gardeners who are willing to garden where they live, no matter how wildly and imaginatively they interpret that principle.

So much of what makes a garden beautiful and satisfying, as well as fragrant, colorful, and productive, is an abundance of healthy plants. No matter what its location or style, the plantings are what give a garden so much of its character as well as its sensuality. Whether plants grow lustily or droop and decline depends on how seriously the gardener has faced up to the realities of his or her own garden situation, studied and understood all the possibilities and limitations, and then taken to heart the mantra of "right plant, right place."

BELOW: *The textural quality of chunky granite walls is set off by stands of skinny, smooth* Equisetum ssp., *commonly known as horsetail, in this sophisticated Balinese garden.*

RIGHT: *A bristly pine and the thick splays of gunnera leaves give a timeless, almost prehistoric quality to a pond's vast smoothness.*

LEFT: *The weeping Higan cherry (*Prunus subhirtella *'Pendula') blooms on the cusp of the spring equinox, the fragility of its pale pink flowers capturing the essence of the season.*

BELOW: *This home's sunroom is grounded to its prairie landscape by a cottage garden of colorful perennials and vines, well suited to the house's casual shingle style.*

RIGHT: *An essentially green garden and wide expanse of stone step and walk create a quiet, serene atmosphere that complements the placidity of the stream running through it.*

NEXT PAGE: *Proportion, style, and transition stem from the relationship between house and garden. The strong lines of sagebrush and other native plants hold their own against the dramatic angularity of this desert home.*

chapter three

SCALE

THE RELATIONSHIP OF GARDEN TO HOUSE:

PATTERNS
OF
SCALE

PATTERNS IN THE GARDEN TRANSCEND STYLE, and this fact is most apparent in the relation of house to garden. While some gardens strictly mirror the architectural style of the houses they surround, that isn't necessary. Such scrupulous consistency between indoors and out is often a hallmark of contemporary homes, perhaps because their architecture is often so distinctive that garden elements are kept sleek and minimal. Since Arts-and-Crafts design elements are so popular and well documented, bungalow-style homes, too, tend to repeat their aesthetic outside their doors. Though such rigor reinforces the home's design, a garden can offer so much more. It can soften, complicate, spark, and otherwise enliven architec-

ture. Simply echoing the style of the house can be a missed opportunity for creativity. While a garden should "go with" the house, it certainly doesn't need to match. Repetition of materials and colors and attention to consistency of scale are other, more subtle ways to ensure pleasant transitions between indoors and out.

In fact, sometimes the house-to-garden dynamic is most interesting when the two are distinctly different in style. Either great drama or tranquility can lie in this

It's difficult to picture this entry without its curtain of Virginia creeper (Parthenocissus quinquefolia), for the vine's appealing drape offers shelter while tying the house's hard materials to the softness of its woodland setting.

A single urn with an eye-catching plant is all it takes to complete the furnishing of a small terrace.

juxtaposition of elements. For instance, while you might expect a country cottage to be surrounded by a flowery cottage-style garden, a more highly designed space with sophisticated materials lends an unexpected, lively quality to the scene. A contemporary home set into a landscape of prairie flowers and grasses is softened in a way that a modernist landscape wouldn't provide.

All of these style considerations play into the patterns you choose to tie your house and garden together. What is

vital is that scale and proportion between the two are of primary consideration, as are the transitions between indoor and outdoor spaces. A harmonious scale is far more important to the ultimate feel of the property than repetition of decorative detail.

PATTERN 1: SCALE

No element in garden design is more elusive to grasp than scale, yet nothing more greatly influences how you feel when in the garden. You know correct scale when you feel it—the trick is figuring out how to create outdoor spaces in harmonious proportion to the home they surround.

Gardeners are usually so busy looking down at the ground, figuring out how to orchestrate layers of plants from large trees down to groundcovers, that we forget to look up to see how the scale of the garden works with the house and with the neighborhood. As we're busy dividing the garden up into rooms with fencing and hedging, we tend to forget about macro-scale—how the garden relates to the house and the larger environment. But if we get this right, we can be confident of creating comfortable and welcoming garden spaces. You can discover clues to understanding your own felt sense of scale by paying close attention to spaces you enjoy and those you don't when you visit gardens, and thinking about why. Perhaps pushing open a large, heavy gate to a garden makes the entry into the space feel rich with portent, or maybe it irritates you with its grandiosity. A winding pathway to the front door may awaken a sense of interest in what is just around the corner; but if its narrowness feels claustrophobic and inhibiting rather than delightful, that's a good clue as to your own felt sense of scale. There's no right or wrong answer, as long as the approach to the front door is safely navigable. But there are personal preferences, interpretations, and enjoyment (or not) to consider—all of which help us determine our own felt sense of garden scale.

The good news is that scale can be easily altered. A broad patio makes the garden feel roomier by visually expanding the groundscape. The addition of a hefty pergola or a tall, pointed tree to guide your eye upward can change how we experience the scale of a garden. And if that pointed tree is used to guide your eye beyond the garden's boundaries to the sea, sky, or neighboring trees beyond, it gives the garden context through the Japanese concept of borrowed scenery. Pruning a hedge to give a

view of a distant vista, echoing the shapes of nearby hillsides with rounded shrubs or boulders in your own garden, or using any other visual device to entice the eye from foreground to background adds this extra dimension to the experience of being in the garden.

It can be fun to play around with scale. By using unexpectedly large objects or especially tiny pieces of garden furniture, you can startle people into paying attention to the garden and taking a closer look around them. Humor can be introduced through such new perceptions of scale. Fill narrow borders with huge plants to create an Alice-down-the-rabbit-hole effect of shrinking the viewer, or make a small garden seem much larger by dividing it into a series of rooms or blurring the boundaries with soft hedging.

*A Japanese stewartia (*Stewartia pseudocamellia*) plays the role of focal point in autumn. Its height lends scale to the pitched roof while anchoring year-round the mixed shrubbery border.*

A pattern in a large garden can be totally self-referential and thus create its very own scale. Picture a raked-sand and stone Zen garden set into a naturalistic landscape, or a fenced children's play area, somewhat separate but still visually connected to the larger garden. In a smaller garden, the owner has no such luxury, as the garden relates so closely to the structure it surrounds. How often have you seen great big houses plopped down on flat lawns, with no connection between the two? In such cases of more house than garden, or when a house is especially tall compared to the dimensions of the garden, creating a workable, comfortable scale is especially important.

Beware the error made most often by nondesigners, which is thinking small when it comes to scale. Whether they're designing a pergola, a walkway, stepping-stones, or a garden shed, people usually err on the side of the diminutive, and thus miss the potential impact and power of these structures. The miss doesn't usually lie in a lack of square footage, but rather in the dimensions of the thing. Garden structures, perhaps because they're outside under the open sky, look best when made hunky and sturdy. Spindly posts, lightweight fencing, too-small stepping-stones, or rickety steps all diminish the garden rather than add to its impact. One reason this happens is that we forget that gardens are always growing, which means that vines will climb those pergola posts and groundcovers will lap at the edges of the walkway. Usually far sooner than we expect,

ABOVE: *A mostly green garden plays off the textural siding and strong forms of this home; the curving path echoes the shape of the front door.*

RIGHT: *Fast-growing, flamboyant tropicals provide instant scale to this Brazilian garden. In temperate climates, we can achieve a similar effect, but it takes a little longer!*

they'll be partially covered. Haven't you all too often seen an arbor pulled askew by a wisteria vine, or a pathway so overgrown as to be nearly impassable? Both make you feel uneasy, slightly worried, uncomfortable. This isn't usually caused by the element's style or materials, but rather by its scale, or lack of it. So out in the garden, it's best to err on the side of sturdiness and heft for any garden structure or element, which in turn allows you to be a little more generous with your plantings. If your site is small, or your house takes up most of the property, it's even more vital to pay close attention to scale. Use fewer elements, but make sure each is as sturdy and large as you can make it. A little garden filled with diminutive elements looks fussy and unimportant. As counterintuitive as it may seem, using generously scaled and sturdy garden elements results in a garden that feels roomier and more comfortable.

The garden at the Getty Center overlooking Los Angeles is a masterful play on scale. The conceptual artist Robert Irwin was charged with making a garden alongside the massive new museum designed by architect Richard Meier. How in the world to compete with such grandeur? Meier himself favored a terrace with a grid of trees, as austere and classical as the building itself. But Irwin took a quite different approach, one that has been criticized by the design world while thoroughly enjoyed by museum visitors. To descend into Irwin's intimate, playful, and quirky garden to find water, color, and a cottage-garden tumble of flowers is to take a step back into familiarity and intimacy for dazed museumgoers overawed by the majesty of Meier's palatial building. People recognize dahlias and roses they remember from their grandmothers' gardens, and relax on benches skirted with fragrant foliages and brightly colored flowers. I wonder if it is too much to say that people regain a sense of self among the flowers,

Art as well as architecture can be used to create garden scale, as in this ten-foot-high bowling ball pyramid, a startling sight nestled among the firs and ferns.

enveloped by a garden in the shadow of one of the grandest and most expensive buildings on earth?

Pattern Consideration: Outbuildings

Scale in the garden is established by more than the house; garden outbuildings can be used to reinforce the scale of the dominant building, or to alter it. Perhaps the most interesting example of this is an iconic one from our agricultural history. Think of the discrepancy in size between a little white farmhouse and a big red barn—it's such a typical scene from America's past. It was the utilitarian barn, usually with a prominently peaked roof, that set the scale for the place.

Today, on our smaller lots, the eye can be brought down from the usually dominant house to garden scale

THE HUMAN HAND

The whole concept of scale is demystified when we remember that measurements have traditionally been based on the human body. Scale is all about being in a space and moving through it. You can envision and describe scale in multiples of human height and width. For example, a horse's height is measured by the length of the human hand, as in "That mare is 12 hands." When we measure just about anything else, it is in terms of inches, feet, and multiples of feet—all of which we can relate to our own bodies. Think about how Japanese houses are traditionally dimensioned around multiples of a tatami mat, which is about 3 by 6 feet, or the space a human being takes up when reclining. This reliance upon our own bodies to make sense of the space around us is why we can most easily comprehend buildings that are "in human scale," or why we enjoy pathways wide enough for two people to walk side by side.

with a gazebo or an open-sided pergola or pavilion. If furniture or a potting bench is visible, human scale is quickly established. Other types of working buildings, albeit on a slightly different scale than a big red barn, can also make a garden more intimate while serving a useful purpose. Greenhouses and garden sheds, whether destinations at the back of the garden, attached to the back or side of the house, or part of a "garden room," effectively alter the scale of the space. They offer a sense of enclosure and purpose to the garden, while their architecture, detail, and paint color give the gardener yet another chance to add style or reinforce the feel of the house.

One of the most charming garden houses I've ever seen was a tiny yoga studio, set into a back corner of the garden. The little peak-roofed house had its own miniature porch with window boxes, a Dutch door, and paned windows. Because it was backed up against a giant fir tree, there was a fairy-tale sense about it that drew you the length of the garden and up onto the porch to peek in the windows. Inside, there was just enough space for a yoga mat, chair, lamp, and bookshelf. The wooden floor gleamed, light poured in, and here the gardener took a break from her labors to read, do asanas, or nap curled up in the chair. If the woman had never set foot in the door, the little house would have been more than worthwhile, for all the plantings in the garden seemed larger and more significant in relationship to it.

Pattern Consideration: Decorative Elements

Another clever manipulation of scale I saw recently was nothing more than an oversized door set into a back fence and painted a deep forest green. I can't tell you how mysterious that doorway looked at the very back corner of the garden. It only opened onto the back alley—but that wasn't the point. Just a door, impressive due to its size and deepness of color, cast a spell, and made one wonder what was on the other side, even though in actuality it was nothing more than the trash cans. I've seen mirrors used in the same way to evoke a sense of mystery. Mounted on a fence or wall, they reflect back the light, or form the dark mouth of a cavern, changing throughout the day with sunlight and shadow. All these manipulations of the size and dimensions of the garden change the felt sense of the space, allowing a visitor to

A FRAGRANT ENTRY

Nothing creates atmosphere and captures attention as surely as catching a sweet scent as we approach the front door. Include fragrant plants in any planting scheme for entry or egress. No matter whether you go in and out the door multiple times a day or are a visitor approaching for the first time, a hit of fragrance is always noticed and appreciated. One large pot can be changed out with fragrant plants through the seasons: a bunching of glossy-leafed little sarcococca for winter, fragrant narcissus for early spring, purple heliotrope or chocolate cosmos for summer into autumn. Or if you have a planter or window box sufficiently roomy for a mix of flowers and shrubs, be sure to tuck a fragrant plant or two around the edges. Just like perfume on the wrist, fragrance in the garden can be layered on for effect. Drape a nearby arbor with *Clematis armandii* for flower and perfume in early springtime, or a wisteria for the ultimate in May fragrance. In summer, growing a stand of lilies nearby, or lining the pathway with lavender, will provide both a colorful approach to the house and a sensual experience for all who pass by.

A roofed and pillared colonnade forms a gradual transition from indoors to out, while providing a sheltered spot from which to enjoy the garden.

enter into the imagination and aesthetics of the gardener while experiencing the garden much more acutely. It is less easy to manipulate scale with architecture that flows out from the house, for whether arbor, pergola, or covered porch, these structures relate directly to the house, whether actually attached or just adjacent. (These elements are discussed more thoroughly in Chapter Five.)

Pattern Consideration: Plantings for Scale

The largest permanent plantings in the garden, usually trees, hedging, and the more massive shrubs, are also vital in setting the scale of house and garden. Think of a tall house where the porch is flanked with the skyward points of Italian cypresses, or perhaps shaded with the tracery of maple branches. After all, we live in a house just part of the time, but in the garden always. It is the garden's trees and larger plantings that should set the scale for the house, not the other way around, as we see most often. Clusters of small trees, such as vine maples or birches near the house, or significant hedging dividing the garden into

ACHIEVING SCALE THROUGH ENTRY

A common pattern from decades past was a straight, narrow paved path leading directly up to the front door from the sidewalk. While this is certainly straightforward, it isn't very interesting and does nothing to integrate house and garden.

Two patterns for an entry garden:

1. A walkway can be further widened visually with low plantings on each side. Such beds also afford a spot to plant interesting low-voltage lighting to enhance the approach both during the day with visual appeal and at night by casting light across the pathway. This scheme enhances an already existing scenario and leaves maximum room for plantings.

2. Even with the smallest property, interest can be created between street and house with the simple addition of a freestanding wall, fence, or screen set a few feet inside the property line. Someone entering then chooses to turn one way toward the driveway, or the other to approach the house. A tree or a small grove of birches seen over the wall lends interest on the street side and privacy to the house and garden inside. This scheme creates two distinct pathways as well as architectural interest and privacy.

distinct rooms, or a massing of shrubbery to enclose certain areas, all bring the sense of scale back into the garden.

Pattern Consideration: Transitions, Entries, and Incidents

Transitions between inside and outside tie the house and garden together, giving us comfort and clarity as we come and go. Plants or architecture can be used to create patterns of bringing a home into scale with the garden. In a formal setting, a pair of 'Skyrocket' junipers (*Juniperus scopulorum* 'Skyrocket') or Italian cypresses (*Cupressus sem-*

How out of scale would this grand façade look with close-to-the-ground foundation plantings, instead of the far more effective coating of evergreen vines and simple row of hefty terra cotta pots?

pervirens) could flank the front porch, their height creating a pleasant transition between the flat ground and the house's eaves. People like to feel some shelter near doorways, and this effect can be accomplished with plants as well as with architecture. Plantings are a softer way to tie house to garden at various entries while contributing a leafy sense of enclosure to the scene. The transition between house and garden is every bit as important at the back of the house or in the side yard as it is in front, even though here it usually involves just the family or a few guests. Generous porches, paving, or decking; a roof or arbor overhead; and steps with sturdy railings and night lighting all make the necessary routine of going in and out more comfortable and significant. Areas for outdoor living are often clustered around the doorway leading from the kitchen or family room, and if this doorway can be glass

Shelves of bonsai and a tile roof hint at the Asian-style delights within the garden walls.

sliders or French doors, or even perhaps a garage door that opens fully to the elements, we have the feel of the outdoors inside on even the hottest or wettest days. On days with more agreeable weather, expanses of glass and doors that open wide encourage us to take a cup of coffee, snack, meal, or magazine out into the garden.

Transparency is the goal of any entry pattern, as you'll appreciate if you've wandered around looking for someone's front door. No matter how gracious or attractive a home's entry might be, the sense of welcome will be lost if it isn't immediately perceivable to a guest approaching the home. A well-placed door, perhaps painted a contrasting color and sheltered by a covered porch, is one traditional

pattern. All entry patterns should include a spacious walkway or clean, sturdy stepping-stones. Overhead protection and night lighting are also important for a sense of safety and security.

But clarity need not require the obvious or expected. Entries are places to play with scale, and set the tone for the rest of the garden. They're a chance to make the house a part of the garden, with the result that both are enhanced. Create interest with an "incident" or two along the way—for example, with screening that directs you around a corner to an intimate patio, or past a pond. No one minds wandering a bit if there is something that catches the attention along the way, particularly if it foreshadows what is to come. For example, a small entry courtyard obscured by a hedge or a painted screen could hold an urn planted up in shades of chartreuse, with the same color scheme repeated on the porch or in the door color. A tall, solid gate gives a sense of entrance, sets the scale for what is to come, and also adds a little mystery to what you might find inside. Just be sure not to curve a pathway around nothing at all, or set up a series of screens that hide … nothing. Make the trip to the door worthwhile with a water feature, plantings, pots, or places to pause. A welcoming pattern for houses that sit above the street is a flight of wide stairs to bring the height of the house into scale. Nice, wide steps invite a rest, or a built-in bench along the way provides a place to set down a package, tie a shoe, or stop a minute.

A wooden pergola lends privacy, creates a shady outdoor room, and links the house to the garden. Its sturdy posts anchor the variety of plantings just outside the door of this 1950's rambler.

PLANTING PATTERNS TO LINK HOUSE TO GARDEN

Typical front-yard planting patterns often utilize a lawn-and-foundation-planting scheme with a flat lawn and mounded shrubs across the front of the house. But this is a missed chance to tie house and garden together. And most shrubs will soon outgrow their space and block the windows, if they don't die first from lack of water beneath the eaves.

Two planting patterns for the front of the house:

1. A tall house can be brought into scale by adding another level or two between eaves and ground. For example, a Japanese maple can shade the porch and soften the exterior of the house; plantings can be moved out away from the house, with a river of rocks under the eaves. This type of scheme is better for security, helps preserve the paint job, and is a practical solution for the dry shade under the eaves, where plants rarely thrive.

2. Extending the front porch into a deck or patio forms a new outdoor living space as well as a gracious entry, particularly when sheltered by an arbor. The arbor can be left as architecture or garnished with a vine for seasonal bloom and fragrance. The paved or decked area offers a place to greet guests, to set down groceries on the way to the kitchen, to sit for a minute, or to display pots filled with flowers and foliage.

FAR LEFT: *The tree's vertical lines give visual relief to all the horizontal walls, terraces, and steps in this interplay of man-made and living forms.*
LEFT: *The simple lines of a rustic wooden bridge contrast with the stone terrace and flower-packed steps to form a surprisingly sophisticated entry.*
BELOW: *A clematis-draped guesthouse brings the eye down from towering conifers to the more intimate, human scale of the garden.*
NEXT PAGE: *This highly atmospheric garden room features art, topiary, and a miniature maze. If you can't recognize and name what it is you love about a certain space, it's impossible to reproduce it in your own home and garden.*

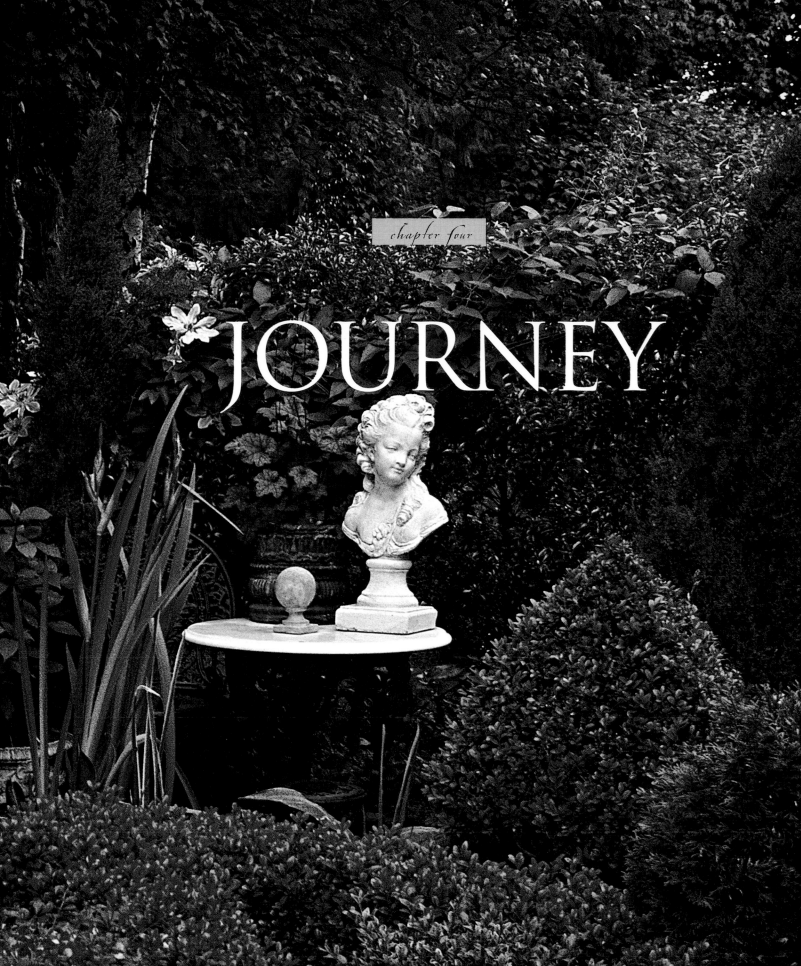

chapter four

JOURNEY

THE GARDEN JOURNEY:

PATTERNS FOR ROOMS, PATHWAYS, BRIDGES, AND GATES

WE EXPERIENCE A GARDEN by moving through it, which is why gazing out the window or even over the fence, let alone at a photograph, is unsatisfactory. Gardens are three-dimensional, and we need to experience ourselves in the space, enjoy it as it unfolds before us, to understand and appreciate a garden. This is why a garden remains the most resonant of journey metaphors, for in a garden it is always more enjoyable to travel than to arrive.

Designing passage through the garden involves practical considerations like night lighting, width of pathways, sturdiness of railings, and safety of steps. But artistic considerations are every bit as important, for it is a sense of mystery and intrigue, the unfolding of delights and vistas, that draws us in to explore the garden. While our feet seek dry and secure passage, our brains and souls seek surprise, stimulation, beauty, and a sense of wonder. The best garden journey involves the imagination every bit as much as the feet. Good design means a careful orchestration of what someone feels, hears, smells, touches, sees, and anticipates while passing through the garden.

Garden rooms, pathways, bridges, and gates are the patterns that facilitate passage through the garden and create a sense of unfolding. These can be thought of either

A birdbath at one end and a shed at the other lead your eyes and feet along the garden path.

Lilies and climbing roses create a scented bower, radiating around a classical fountain and enclosed by walls of boxwood hedging.

as simple constructions or as iconic pieces rich with meaning, depending on the day and the task. As I'm hauling a bag of heavy soil through a gate, or trundling a heavy wheelbarrow along a path, I'm thinking only of their width, utility, and the ease of passage they afford. When I click open the garden gate first thing on a frosty morning or cross a little bridge in a more meditative frame of mind, these simple garden elements evoke moving from one realm to another, leaving something behind while moving on to a new reality, if only for a moment. These patterns can be added to any garden, not only to make passage pleasant, easy, and safe but also to further the chance that we'll experience the garden on a variety of different levels, depending on the day, the weather, and the mood.

PATTERN 2: GARDEN ROOMS

The idea of "garden rooms" might seem too formal or even intimidating. Perhaps the term calls interior design to mind, with visions of decorating and accessorizing. Or maybe it evokes impressive English estates featuring mossy old stone or brick walls far more venerable than anything on this side of the ocean. We remember the mystery of the unattainable lost room in *The Secret Garden,* and we think of garden rooms on a scale far grander than would apply to our urban, suburban, or even rural properties.

But creating garden rooms is nothing more than a method of dividing and connecting areas of garden space. Because garden rooms have entrances, they're an effective way to create anticipation and the feel of unfolding space as we pass through the garden. If we get used to the idea that every garden room need not be designated with a special use—rose garden, kitchen garden, furnished space for outdoor living, and so on—it expands the possibilities. Rather, garden rooms are simple divisions of outdoor space based on topography, aesthetics, architecture, or function—and in the best garden rooms, all four elements come into play.

Dividing a garden into rooms allows us to recapture the scale of a garden and bring it down to human size, drawing walls about us so that we feel cozier in the spaces, despite the open-air ceiling. Garden rooms create intimacy and comfort in being outdoors. The walls, hedging, fencing, or other devices used to create garden rooms can be as impermeable or as transparent as we like. Although some garden rooms are clearly separate spaces delineated by solid walls, others are created with mere suggestions of division. Counterintuitively, when garden space is divided up into rooms, even the smallest property seems larger, as you're drawn from one "doorway" to the next to see what each space contains.

The whole concept of garden rooms is an elastic one, unrestrained by the need for wallboard, roof, ductwork, or any of the other necessities of indoor living. All you're doing is playing with space, dividing it up in ways that suit how you live outdoors and how you plan to plant up spaces. Or perhaps you're working around already established beds and borders. No matter. Vary the size, entry, exit, and materials according to use and topography. A garden room can be anything from a little fence corralling a sea of colorful perennials, to a dining pavilion, to a courtyard linking wings of a house. It can be formed by a pergola overhead, by paving underfoot, by plants that grow up to create a screen, by serious walls, or by a partial gesture of a fence.

Pattern Consideration: Purpose

Each garden room should feel distinct and purposeful. Whether the use is obvious, like an entryway, a courtyard linking rooms, or a parking area, or whether the purpose is less clear, as with a side yard or a street-buffering space, each garden room is an opportunity to create individual atmosphere within the greater garden. A patio sited where the sun lingers for most of the day, a deck off the kitchen for morning coffee, a shady corner strung with a hammock, or a little herb garden—each space has its own focus or clear reason for being.

The focal point of each space can be artistic, like a decorated mirror on the wall to reflect the plantings in the space, or functional, like a built-in grill in an outdoor

Sometimes subtracting decorative elements has a greater impact than adding more: The smooth expanse of intense wall color plays up the agave's graphic silhouette without need of further embellishment.

The ultimate outdoor room, roofed and wired, furnished with a rug, bed, reading light, and a view out to Lake Whatcom.

kitchen. For that sunny patio, a chaise with colorful cushions could serve as a focal point; often the beds of an herb garden radiate from a central fountain or sundial. A garden room can be created as a backdrop for a piece of sculpture, with all paths leading to that central focus and all plantings chosen to harmonize with it. A cozy space for stargazing calls out for a fire pit. A shady corner in which to read a book or have a private conversation needs comfortable chairs and a side table to hold cups of tea. Such a room beckons as an invitation to sit and enjoy—and even if a busy gardener has little chance to accept such an invitation, the very idea is relaxing. As simple as a bench in a

corner, or as grand as a paved courtyard centered with a splashing fountain, distinct rooms not only lead us through the garden but create reasons to stay put and settle in.

Pattern Consideration: Dividing Lines

The walls, fences, hedges, pots, and plants that serve to divide a garden up into rooms themselves offer an opportunity for color, texture, and embellishment. A smooth gray concrete wall sets the tone of sleek modernism. Stain that wall a ruddy red and you've warmed up the garden, stain it cobalt blue and you've electrified the space. Heavy walls, especially of brick or stone, give instant patina and lend a feeling of age and permanence to even the newest garden. How much the atmosphere of one garden room bleeds into another depends upon the transparency or solidity of what divides them.

And, of course, walls and fences can be considered blank canvases, to be topped with arbors, coated with vines, or hung with art. They form an ideal backdrop for planting beds, support lax plants, and provide a way to incorporate art into the fabric of the garden through their materials or garnishes. A chain link fence, the most utilitarian of ways to divide space, can become a living wall of green when threaded with wisteria.

PATTERN 3: PATHWAYS

When I set to work on my hillside garden many years ago, my first priority was to be able to walk everywhere around the garden on any day of the year and stay clean and dry. It was this simple and practical consideration of what was needed so that I could get outside and cut flowers for the house, every morning if I chose, that drove the whole design of the place. This single-minded focus on clear and easy passage was the impetus for patios, walkways, stepping-stones, gravel paths, and steps. It caused me to vary the materials I used so that walking around the garden would stay interesting. I added curves, corners, gates, and arbors so I'd be sure to slow down, pause, look closely, and appreciate all that was going on, from ground level to overhead.

Though walls, fences, and major plantings, often called the "bones" of the garden, may be the fundamental building blocks of garden design, we experience a garden through its navigability. It is the network of pathways that defines what we see, and whether we enjoy a garden to its fullest or feel frustrated that we couldn't really penetrate its depths. It's obvious that a path should extend to a patio in the back corner, or that steps need to span the garden's levels, but what about a way to reach all those tiny delights in the garden? Many of the garden's greatest treasures are small, and often bloom at times when the

The formality of wide brick steps and low walls is offset by the rough and irregular shelter of tree trunks.

garden is at its coldest and soggiest. Perhaps stepping-stones to a patch of *Iris reticulata* or snowdrops, or a path that leads beneath a witch hazel's fragrant winter bloom, will bring every bit as much pleasure as a firm, poured pad in the utility area.

The discrepancy at the heart of pathway design is as contradictory as human nature. We want a path that gets us where we're going as quickly and in as straightforward a manner as possible; at the same time, we don't really want to see the end of the path when we first put foot to paver. We don't want to look up to see all that lies ahead, any more than we want to know the ending of a novel or a movie before we spend time reading or watching.

Here's the conundrum: while at the most basic level efficient passage is the intent of any path, in our hearts we prefer a bit of enigma, the puzzlement of a garden at least partly obscured. Since the function of a path is to lead us from here to there, curves, obstructions, and surprising

Who could resist traveling this curvaceous trail, lapped with russet-toned Anemanthele lessoniana *and ending in a mysterious yew-hedged circle at the edge of the forest?*

destinations must appear uncontrived, integral to the design. So wind a pathway around a tree, hide a tea table and chair at the farthest point of a dead end, train trees or vines to meet overhead, or place scrim plants to obscure a bend in the road—but never, ever forget where the path is leading. The intent remains the same no matter the jogs and distractions along the way.

One pattern is a straight shot along a pathway from gate or sidewalk to the front door, perhaps framed by low hedging or flowerbeds. Such a pathway needs to be wide, but not too wide. Enough width for two people to walk comfortably side by side is a good measure (4 to 5 feet for main paths, a minimum of 3 feet for secondary ones), and the wider the pathway the more interest is needed at ground level. If your walkway is crafted in an interesting pattern of natural stone, it can be wider than if it's poured concrete. The walkway will feel narrower if it's hedged on each side, even with only knee-high boxwood or lavender. In contrast, a sea of low-growing groundcover flanking the walkway visually expands the space.

Pathways are far more than just their materials, length, or shape; you have only to navigate the stepping-stones and wander the atmospheric paths of a Japanese garden to appreciate the full effect of artful walkways. In Chinese gardens, the paths are designed to reveal the landscape by degrees, winding and turning so that the garden slowly unrolls and rerolls like a scroll painting.

Pattern Consideration: Mixing of Materials

One uniform material, no matter how lovely, probably doesn't fit all garden situations equally well. Using a single material for paths misses the chance to stir up some excitement and interest underfoot, as well as the opportunity to cue the garden experience by slowing or accelerating one's passage through it.

The most artful walkways compel our feet as well as draw our eyes.

Pathway materials can and should be varied, provided that affinity of color, texture, and basic nature is kept in mind. Gardens can have gravel pathways, with pavers set into the gravel in some areas. Other paths can consist of stones laid stepping distance apart, surrounded by groundcovers. These can widen to areas of cut-stone paving. If the stones are laid out so that the joints form regular patterns, the effect is more formal. If laid out in the Japanese manner, where the joints form only T or L shapes, the effect is asymmetric and more casual. Stone can be fashioned and combined in ways from imposingly solid to seemingly random. Cobbles are all about patterning, while smooth river stones can be set into concrete for an attractively haphazard effect. Or stepping-stones can lead to paving, then to poured aggregate, or perhaps to colored and stamped concrete steps and patios that in turn nudge up against wooden decking. Such a continuum of hard surfaces makes it possible to walk to the farthest corner of a garden on an unmucky surface on any day of the year, while varying the experience according to each area's use and the garden's topography.

Materials underfoot give clues as to how to enjoy the garden. A paver or a flat stone large enough to stand on comfortably with both feet gives a reason to pause and look around. A pathway of small stones or pavers, or a narrow, winding path requires you to slow down and take in what is happening along the way. If there are lovely ferns, mossy stones, or fragrant flowers in bloom beside the path, you'll be sure to notice.

Pathways also afford a chance to embed art into the garden's structure. From an expanse of pebble mosaic that is not only texturally lovely but can give you a foot reflexology treatment as you walk across it, to mosaic pavers embedded in a patio, durable color art underfoot brings an added dimension to garden enjoyment. When art becomes the very fabric of the garden itself, an integral part of the structure, it becomes a far more meaningful part of the garden than when used simply as decoration.

WIDTH OF PASSAGE

Though it's true that the width of a path should vary according to its use, it seems that gardeners never make pathways quite wide enough. The problem is that before the plants grow in, an adequately sized path can look as wide open as a German autobahn. It's charming to have ornamental grasses and groundcovers tumble over and soften the edges, but only if you can still walk past, which is the whole point, after all. Three feet wide is usually substantial enough for an intimate pathway, but think carefully about how thickly you plan to plant the margins. One solution is to visually expand a narrow paved pathway with a wide ribbon of gravel or rock on each side, which softens the hard surface while creating more open space through which to travel. Think about the space needed for two people to walk side by side (4 to 5 feet), and make that a minimum width for main pathways. Then narrow it down where you want the path to wind a bit and draw the garden visitor along.

PATTERN 4: BRIDGES

Count Marcello inhaled deeply. "How do you see a bridge?"

"Pardon me?" I asked. "A bridge?"

"Do you see a bridge as an obstacle—as just another set of steps to climb to get from one side of a canal to the other? We Venetians do not see bridges as obstacles. To us bridges are transitions. We go over them very slowly. They are part of the rhythm. They are the links between two parts of a theater, like changes in scenery, or like the progression from Act One of a play to Act Two. Our role changes as we go over bridges. We cross from one reality … to another reality. From one street … to another street. From one setting … to another setting."

—JOHN BERENDT, *The City of Falling Angels*

Bridges are a powerful metaphor, a symbol of connection and passage. Bridges divide and differentiate garden spaces while creating compelling focal points. They aid navigability, bring architectural elements outdoors, and serve as landings from which to view the rest of the garden. Have you ever seen a bridge that you didn't long to cross? (Well, maybe not one of those swaying suspension bridges.) And because bridges are architectural objects with so many possibilities for color, shape, and design,

they offer a sure way to enhance or confirm the style of any garden, from rustic to contemporary.

Too often bridges are strictly interpreted as arches over water and are relegated to Asian gardens. It is those elaborately ornamented, lacquered, and stylized constructions that we picture when we think of garden bridges. This shows how effectively bridges are used in Asian gardens, where water's reflective qualities are taken full advantage of to double a bridge's impact. But bridges can easily be incorporated into many types of gardens, for in truth a bridge is simply a construction that spans whatever is difficult or impossible to directly cross—be it water, mud, bog, chasm, low spot, or a river of stones.

Pattern Consideration: Materials and Forms

Depending upon construction material and shape, garden bridges range from utilitarian log planks to grandiose lidded arcs. Whether they're a sleek slab of stone or a curvaceously steep arch, there's great latitude in design, depending on style and on what the bridge is spanning. Perhaps because bridges by their very nature excite the imagination, they've

No matter their material or style, bridges stir our imagination with their symbolism of connection and passage.

long been fanciful in both form and ornamentation. The zigzag stone bridge was a classic Chinese shape, designed to prevent evil spirits—believed to be able to move only in straight lines—from crossing over the bridge. Scrollwork railings, brightly lacquered wood, and intricate designs have also long been inspired by the opportunity for reflection from water below, thus emphasizing the design details.

Even a narrow bridge affords the chance to pause, gaze down or out, catch a breath, acknowledge the transition from one side to another. A bridge can be just wide enough for one person to walk across holding on to the rails. Proportion is key—if a bridge is longer, it can be made wide enough so that two or more people can stroll along together, or to allow for sitting and relaxing partway across for a more leisurely experience. Whether a bench is built into the railing or a bridge widens enough in the middle to hold several chairs, its height and unique vantage point offers a special view of the rest of the garden.

Even this simple platform bridge introduces architecture into the garden while affording safe passage across a watery bog.

At its most pared-down form, a bridge can be simply a series of stepping-stones or pavers raised above the level of whatever they are crossing. This minimalist arrangement affords passage while intruding as little as possible on the visual expanse of water, marsh, mud, or bog. It also means that whoever is crossing becomes an active participant, for hopscotching across requires a degree of both nerve and athleticism.

Pattern Consideration: Placement and Safety

Whether a minimalist design or an elaborate one appeals to you and suits the style of your garden, it is worthwhile searching out a spot where you might add a bridge. Opportunities will present themselves when you realize that all you need are two shores or banks, be they flanking a river of stones, a pond, or a shallow dip in topography. Even a suggestion of depth allows the need for a span to cross over it. Safety factors such as height, sturdiness, a nonslip surface, and handrails need to be considered in any design scheme for a bridge. But most important is to get beyond the idea that you need a traditional arch of bridge over a koi pond, which is certainly beautiful but not a requirement. Most gardens have some area you'd prefer not to step into or through. Or it's possible to create a rush of stream water, a pond, or a river of rocks or plantings that cries out for some kind of bridge to cross over it.

PATTERN 5: GATES

A gate is the portal to the garden, and its style sets the tone. The process of passing in and out of the garden can feel as significant as crossing over a bridge—with the added advantage of a satisfying click as the gate closes behind you. Even the simplest of gates can be designed to conceal, to shut off and protect, or to frame views into the garden. The childhood image of hanging on the gate to peer through, or standing on tiptoe to get a glimpse of what Eden lies just beyond, is a powerful one.

My new garden is a tiny one, yet I've squeezed in three gates, which are more important to the garden experience than the fences they connect. Every time I open, pass through, and close a gate it defines the garden for me, making its inner and outer spaces more significant and distinctive. Whether I simply open the side gate to empty the garbage, swing the utility gate to grab the wheelbarrow, or go out the back gate into the lane and leave the garden behind, each one calls attention to the everyday passages that make up my routine.

Gates at the perimeter of the garden, as well as those between garden rooms, reinforce the pleasure of moving in and out of spaces. Inner space protected by a gate feels like private, personal space, even a sanctuary. And when we step outside the gate, we face the world. Leaving the gate wide open invites the world in; closing it firmly behind us shuts it out. The inner and outer realms, whatever you feel those to be on any given day, can be defined by the opening and closing of a garden gate. And, of course, gates serve the practical purposes of privacy and containment. Years ago my husband built a sturdy lattice gate, with open square spaces that were handsome, yet so large that our Scottie could squeeze out. Escape prevention outweighed design considerations, and he installed crosspieces on the bottom squares to keep the dog safely at home in the back yard.

Pattern Consideration: Style and Materials

At a time, and in a country, where gates were far grander than they are now, Gertrude Jekyll wrote in her book *Garden Ornament*: "Overstatement and understatement are alike undesirable . . . An honest relation must exist between the entry and what is entered." Because a gate hints at what lies within, stirring up excitement, anticipation, or even caution, Jekyll felt a gate should present a straightforward clue to what was to come once you entered.

While it's true that a gate sets the mood for the garden, this can be seen as an opportunity for fun, art, or mystery as much as for consistency. Gates are an architectural element in the garden, a chance to emphasize the style of the house, play off it, or be a design element all their own. A gate should be in scale with the property and with the fence or hedge that surrounds it, and in a style that fits comfortably with the house and garden. A heavy, solid gate with a big brass knocker sets up the idea that a very serious garden lies just inside. But perhaps it only means that the gate adjoins a busy road so the family wanted a privacy buffer, and inside the visitor finds an exuberant cottage garden or a wild garden of native plants. An ornamented, curlicued metal gate is more decoration than privacy screen, but nonetheless it gives all the psychological benefits of emphasizing entry and exit while keeping animals and kids inside and intruders out. And its transparency is every bit as tantalizing whether the garden inside is as grand as the gate itself, or a more typical back yard with a vegetable plot and a children's sandpit.

A gate can appear organic, part of the very fabric of the garden. This is especially true of arbor-topped gates draped in vines, rough-hewn log gates, or Japanese bamboo gates held together with ties. Or a gate can be so flat and nonornamented as to blend into the fence completely, with its hinges the only clue to where the fence ends and the gate begins. Gates are effective set into a hedge, where their textural qualities of rough wood or smooth metal stand out against the living twigginess or leafiness of the hedge. When a gate is capped with an arbor or a roof, the experience of entering the garden is enhanced as you walk through shadow back into sunlight.

Gates and doors set the mood and style of the garden, as in this romantic, slightly hobbit-like scene.

MOON GATES

A moon gate is an example of a style ripe with meaning yet adaptable to any garden. The idea of drawing the moon down into the garden, of capturing moonglow and moonrise, stirs us now as it did centuries ago when moon gates were important garden iconography. Originating in China two hundred years before the birth of Christ, early moon gates were simply solid gates pierced by a circular cutout, believed to bestow good luck on anyone who passed through. These days, a moon gate is likely to be as charming as a Dutch door, usually made of solid boards on the bottom half, with a circle cut into the top half. This circular shape is the Buddhist symbol of infinity, and was meant to inspire meditation and contemplation. It also works as a frame to offer a unique view into the garden or out onto the world.

RIGHT: *This near-transparent metal access is more art object than traditional gate, yet it works to stop the eye, define space, and set a modern tone.*

BELOW: *A now suburban garden suggests its rural past with the mere suggestion of a mossy old wooden fence.*

FAR UPPER RIGHT: *A brightly painted ladder-like form serves as both a useful and decorative object, while also evoking an old-fashioned agrarian style.*

FAR LOWER RIGHT: *A darkly secretive-looking gate set into a tall, thick hedge sends out Halloween vibes year-round. It takes courage to ring the entry bell at this threshold!*

NEXT PAGE: *Archetypal ideas and longings, like those for privacy and shelter, can be translated into specific elements that make gardens more than the sum of their plants.*

chapter five

ENCLOSURE

ENCLOSURE AND EXPOSURE:

PATTERNS FOR
SHELTER AND
BORDERS

IT IS OUR INTUITIVE SENSE OF SHELTER that most influences how immediately comfortable we feel in a garden. We may not obviously look around for a solid stretch of fence, an arbor overhead, or a sturdy hedge, but it is these elements that make us relax, enjoy, and feel secure or not. Is there an arbor to soften the sun's glare? Is there a fence to stop the eye and prevent passersby from looking in, or is the garden so wide open that its borders flow into the surrounding neighborhood? Is there a snug courtyard between wings of the house, or does the garden embrace an outward view? A garden usually offers experiences of both exposure (to our surroundings and to the elements) and enclosure (in the form of shelter, refuge, and privacy).

Humans were hunters for eons, and we still respond to a panorama that offers a wide and sweeping vista. We instinctively scan the horizon. Castles were built atop the tallest hill to look out over the countryside, the better to spot approaching danger. We still enjoy the feeling that we get when we're at the highest point and can command a view of all that lies below or before us.

Unfortunately, this urge to see out has resulted in too many front gardens without any sense of delineation, pri-

As open and transparent as this arbor is, its overhead arch clearly delineates the garden's entrance. It lends scale to the flat ground and, when paired with the smaller trellis, creates a rhythm of curves and height.

vacy, or individuality. How many American suburbs appear to be composed of one front lawn after another? Front gardens that flow from one to the other are often largely wasted space, inhabited only when the owners are out mowing, edging, or pruning. Can you imagine pulling a chaise onto the middle of a flat, open front lawn and settling in for a cup of tea or a visit with a friend? You'd feel so exposed. Picture again pulling that same lawn chair into a secluded courtyard, or beneath a shady arbor, and imagine the contentment you'd feel settling into such a sheltered space.

A front courtyard garden is both connected and separate from the street: The open latticework fence invites looking in and out, but its height and darkness create a barrier.

We also crave privacy and shelter in our gardens, for our ancestors lived in caves, huddled around fires, with their backs to the walls for a sense of protection. Today we don't worry about saber-toothed tigers, but we do seek respite from a hectic, noisy, and still unsafe world. Hedges and fences define our private spaces, courtyards lend a strong sense of enclosure, and arbors or pergolas create a canopy for the garden. All these elements provide the structure needed to support and contain plantings and to shape space, as well as extending architecture out into the garden.

PATTERN 6: SHELTERS

The terms "arbor" and "pergola" are often used interchangeably, but in fact they describe shelter structures of

A roofed, columned porch provides a spot to sit that's slightly removed, yet still part of the garden. House is linked to garden, here, by the height of the wooden pergola and the plantings that echo the column forms.

different shapes, if similar utility. The confusion comes because garden history is long, and borrows freely from a variety of traditions, cultures, and styles. No wonder there's a lack of consistency in how these terms are used.

Arbors were originally made to support shrubs and vines, most often grapes. No matter what its purpose, an arbor is a structure with an openwork top that encloses and defines space. Arbors differ from trellises, which are simply lattice structures built for the sole purpose of supporting and training vines and other climbers, and not meant to be walked beneath.

A pergola is perhaps best defined as a colonnade or gallery, usually supported by a double row of columns, most often flat-roofed. A solid wall or fence can form one side, and a pergola's shape is usually linear. The effect is of an enclosure made to walk through, although certainly a pergola can be used for dining or can contain benches for sitting. A lengthy pergola is ideal for linking different parts of the garden and displaying a variety of overlapping vines to create a rhythm of shade and sunlight. The light shed through the structure's canopy can be modulated by how closely the beams are set, and which vines, if any, are grown on the top. Most times such human-made canopies are more garden-friendly than nature's own, for the shade cast by conifers or other evergreen trees is usually dense and dark overhead, while being so dry and rooty at ground level that it is difficult to grow plantings beneath.

What arbors and pergolas most significantly have in common is that they partially put a lid on the garden, bring down the canopy for a stronger sense of being sheltered and protected outside. They serve as a link between indoors and out, a bridge between the house and the natural world. Whether freestanding or attached (but especially the latter), they anchor the garden to the house. They make sense and shape of space and sky.

I became obsessed with garden structures and their potential for enchantment because of an arbor. Many years ago, on a warm, rainy May morning, I stood beneath a vast arbor at Coker Arboretum in Chapel Hill, North Carolina. The group I was with clustered beneath the 200-foot-long arbor, looking up into long, purple racemes of headily fragrant wisteria that covered the arbor and dripped bounteously down through the roof. This sensory overload was composed simply of wooden supports, lattice overhead, and a venerable vine in bloom—a combination we can all create, at whatever scale works best, in our own gardens. The size of the arbor, as well as its construction, location, cost, or material, mattered not at all. Such a memorable experience was created simply by a flowering vine supported so sturdily overhead that we felt comfortable standing beneath and looking up. A vine-free arbor can have nearly as much impact, for its openwork design makes each passing cloud, the stars, and the moon appear framed, as if offering a special and intimate celestial peep show.

Arbors and pergolas offer shade, shelter, enclosure, and patterning of light and dark in the garden. The experience of being outdoors is greatly enhanced by having a roof over some portion of the garden, for only when you come out from under an arbor and look up do you really appreciate how high and open the sky is. You're drawn into a garden by the chance to stand under a porch roof and look out, or for the pleasure of walking out of the sunshine into the cool, leafy shade of a vine-draped arbor or pergola. One of the very greatest lures for walking through a garden is this patterning of full sun, dappled light, or shadows, all effects created by such structures. Since Roman times, arbors have been constructed off in far corners as destinations worth walking the length of the garden to experience.

Both arbors and pergolas are at heart garden follies, fun buildings with shape, form, and embellishment limited only by their constructor's imagination. They can be airy or vine-draped, or made rhythmic by building several in staggered or intermittent patterns. When paved and furnished, they form open-air outdoor rooms ideal for entertaining and dining, or as a quiet retreat for reading or napping. Their roofs can be vaulted, partial, sloped, or peaked. They can be attached to the house to create an extended roofline out into the garden; such structures are ideal vehicles for reinforcing the design and materials of the house, extending these elements into the outdoors. Or they can be something quite separate from the house, relating only to the garden in style, creating a whole different feeling outside.

BELOW: *An old-fashioned gazebo is a glamorous focal point, making any garden feel like an estate from the last century, no matter its size or style of planting.*

RIGHT: *A glossy urn and carved Indonesian furnishings add complexity to a simple planting of fancy-leafed geraniums.*

LEFT: *While most courtyards are integral to a home's architecture, they can also be created out in the landscape with paving, hedging, and fencing.* ABOVE: *Branches of an old apple tree shelter a colorful chair and table that draw you in to sit down, relax, and enjoy this private little space.*

An arbor or a pergola can be a focal point, topped with elaborate beams, painted bright colors, built of rustic peeled posts, or its roof can be glassed or draped in shimmery, floating fabric. Or it can be a more humble structure, a tiny nook sheltering only a bench, a chair, or even a woodpile.

You don't need to look far to find the perfect place for such a structure in most gardens. Walkways, patios, terraces, transitions, and passageways all might benefit from a lid. Any wall of the house can be embellished with an attached arbor; and when an arbor extends over a doorway it offers a welcome sheltered place for digging out keys or setting down bags of groceries. Any sunny spot where you'd like to grow a vine or two, or a destination spot in the garden, as well as any location where you'd like to create a seating area, is a potential site. Walk slowly through the garden, look up, and think about where patterns of shade and sunlight might be welcome. Sooner or later, most of us run out of ground space in our gardens, while the vertical space goes untapped. Arbors and pergolas create three-dimensional gardening space as well as shade and shelter.

Whether left bare as an architectural feature, furnished as open-air living space, or planted with vines for fragrance, flower, leaf, or food, such structures catch the eye while injecting the garden with style and substance. Arbors and pergolas can be sleekly modern, twiggily rustic, made of hunky stone or brick, or curved like a tunnel. They can lead from one part of the garden to another, define an outdoor room, or create a destination. You can play around with style and utility, but what is most vital in the design of these structures is that they be sturdy and in scale with what is around them. Arbors, through their own strength and integrity, can transform a garden space from ordinary to significant and make memorable the garden experience.

Pattern Consideration: Courtyards

A courtyard creates the most intimate and secure of outdoor spaces, for it's usually enclosed, or mostly so, by the bulk and solidity of house and garage or other major structures. No other exterior space relates so closely to the architecture and atmosphere of the house. This effect can be furthered when flooring, such as concrete, brick, or stone, runs continuously from the inside rooms out into the courtyard, effectively blurring the lines between exterior and interior. Perhaps because of their European tradition and connotations, and because we don't see them as often as we should in our own architecture, courtyards have a unique cachet and charm. Whether grandly colonnaded, centered with a gushing fountain, or tiny and cobbled, courtyards feel warm, sheltered, enveloping, and comfortable. They provide the most gentle of transitions possible between indoors and out.

urban and suburban properties. In American suburbs, where one garden often flows into the neighboring ones, courtyards can create privacy; in the city, they are secure and private spaces away from the bustle of the streets. There's no better way to ensure privacy, as well as safety and refuge, than by putting part of a building between your garden and the outside world.

Even on the smallest property, it may be possible to push the outside walls of the house as close to the property line as allowable to create space for an interior courtyard. Such construction enhances indoor living as well, for light is brought directly into the core of the house. When a home is built to wrap around a courtyard, the result is livable outdoor space as well as a greater connection between nature and all the rooms that open or look out on the courtyard. In cooler, wetter climates, a courtyard can bring light, sky, and weather in for as close an experience

of nature as you're likely to find from inside the house. Entry courtyards can be formed with fences and hedging, and a series of courtyards provides a sense of entry that becomes more private as you progress from the street to the front door.

PATTERN 7: BORDERS

Our gardens are made distinct and separate by fencing or hedging. Whether man-made or living green, solid or nearly transparent, these boundaries outline our gardens, articulate property lines, create privacy and security. How often have you heard that good fences make good neighbors? Robert Frost's poem "Mending Wall" is as true

Fencing and gates are as much about invitation as about privacy and delineation.

today as when it was written. As lot sizes shrink and our society becomes more litigious, the demarcation provided by clear property lines is vital. Whether a thickly impenetrable yew hedge or a 4-foot woven screen separating apartment balconies, the impulse for definition and division is the same, as is the effect of whatever material is used to delineate boundaries.

Our felt sense of enclosure and exposure takes on more relevance and even perhaps urgency when it comes to fencing and hedging. Have you ever pitied one of those poor dogs sitting in his yard looking glumly out at nothing, longing to scamper and explore but knowing full well that an "invisible fence" will give him an electric shock if he puts one paw over the boundary? That look of confusion and inhibition is one we all understand when the lines between public and private property, or those between neighbors, aren't clearly defined. It's only by having a fence or hedge to pass through to get to the outside world that we appreciate the security and privacy within. What type of material you choose, living or artificial, solid or transparent, high or low, depends on the style of your home and garden, how much space you have, your aesthetics, and whether you need instant results or can wait for a hedge or hedgerow to grow in.

Pattern Consideration: Fences and Screens

Fences are continuous, connected, and usually opened with a gate, while screens are more often freestanding, partial, fragmentary. Both serve essentially the same purpose, except that you usually can't keep a dog or child in, or strangers out, with a screen. Both fences and screens create privacy; interrupt, block, or frame views; serve as backdrop and scaffolding for plantings; and provide outline and definition; but only fences secure property.

There are countless styles of fences, from closely set boards that act as a solid wall, to transparent panels of glass or Plexiglas. In between are metal fencing (gracefully curvaceous or rigidly intimidating), open latticework or

Stone brings a sense of age and stolidity to even the most extravagantly planted garden, as with these hunky stone arbors trimmed in ivy.

wire fencing ideal for growing vines, old-fashioned pickets, or down-home post and rail. An English wattle fence is comfortably rustic, while chain link is so utilitarian it cries out for a tumbling twine of clematis or at least a sleeve of woven reeds. The choice of material depends on the job to be done. Height, length, sturdiness, and degree of transparency are the main considerations.

Setting a fence back a bit from the curb or road so that there is a planting bed outside as well as inside is a way to capture more garden space as well as to soften the fence. Topping it with a trellis adds height and interest. Fences don't need to be solid to provide some privacy; pickets and galvanized, heavy-gauge hogwire, for example, stop the eye while allowing light and air to pass through. And a fence need not be a straight line; it can undulate with the curves of the land, or can be built with nooks and crannies to hold potted plantings or pieces of art.

Since fencing is often the first thing a visitor sees, style is important. A mid-twentieth-century house sided in zinc would look incongruous surrounded by a picket fence, just as a casual shingled cottage would look odd fenced in spiky, Gothic wrought iron. But often sympathy of style is more interesting than consistency of style. For instance, that same shingled cottage would appear distinguished fenced in cedar-trimmed hogwire laced with vines, or perhaps with latticework painted celadon green or deepest gray. The smooth, sophisticated contemporary house might be softened with the texture and history of a Japanese bamboo fence; or if it's particularly blessed with expanses of glass, it might benefit from the privacy of a sleek and simple fence of closely set boards.

Pattern Consideration: Hedges

From the outside, evergreen hedging appears sturdy, peaceful, established, formal. From the inside, such deeply green, textural, living walls create a quiet, private garden as well as a perfect backdrop against which to show off colorful and varied plantings. Too often in American gardens, though, evergreens are pulled back from the street to encompass the house in foundation plantings. Doesn't it make more sense to push those plantings out to corral private, functional space for gardening and outdoor living? Hedging can also work well within gardens as well as around their perimeters, for it can consist of knee-high boxwood balls as well as sky-high yews. Within gardens, hedging is a soft, green way to divide space into rooms, line walkways, delineate herb gardens or flower beds, screen off utility areas, or create privacy anywhere you need it. I've even seen herb beds outlined in little chive hedges.

Predictable plants, such as photinia, laurel, and Leyland cypress, are overused for hedging because they grow quickly (often so quickly as to be difficult to maintain) and are sturdily evergreen. But there are so many more interesting choices with colored foliages and fragrant flowers that it is a shame to stick to the familiar. And even predictable choices can be made interesting through pruning: I've seen glossy laurel regimentally clipped into a flat, dark curtain to serve as backdrop for a little grove of white-barked birches. It is a beautiful sight. Most evergreens will work well when routinely clipped flat like a living curtain—which also saves on garden space. Just be sure to check the eventual size of any shrub or tree in your climate before planting.

For a hedge of a neighborly height, choose plants that naturally top out at 4 feet or so, such as the fragrant, white-blooming *Osmanthus delavayi* with tiny, dark green leaves. Other useful low-growing hedging plants are glossy, easily clipped boxwood (*Buxus* spp.) and its lookalike Japanese holly (*Ilex crenata*). Boxleaf honeysuckle (*Lonicera nitida* 'Baggesen's Gold') has yellow leaves. For a less formal look, you might try Indian hawthorn (*Rhaphiolepis indica*) or an upright rosemary like 'Tuscan Blue', for its aromatic foliage that's ideal to clip for soups or casseroles. *Escallonia* 'Apple Blossom' is slightly tender, but forms a lushly blooming hedge of pink flowers in warmer gardens. No plant has a richer, darker green sheen than yew, a traditional, but not quite expected, hedging plant; *Taxus* x *media* 'Brownii' has a dense, rounded shape that naturally grows to only about 8 feet tall.

For hedges tall and thick enough to ensure privacy, Pacific wax myrtle (*Myrica californica*) and Canada hemlock (*Tsuga canadensis*) have interesting textures. The taller species of Oregon grape (*Mahonia aquifolium*) form a wild-looking hedge with spikes of yellow winter flowers. For another winter-blooming hedge, the slightly tender

Perhaps the ultimate expression of plants as architecture, these hornbeams have been pruned into gothic-like cathedral windows framing beds that burst with poppies, fennel, and allium.

The ephemeral, elegant drippiness of white wisteria on the arbor contrasts with the year-round evergreen forms of topiary and hedging.

(to zone 7) *Viburnum tinus* 'Spring Bouquet' forms a fat, fragrant evergreen wall. Or you can get creative or elaborate with your hedging: at Heronswood Nursery near Kingston, Washington, European hornbeams (*Carpinus betulus* 'Fastigiata') have been pruned into a rhythmic series of vaulted cathedral windows for hedging that cleverly divides, while it frames and reveals.

Pattern Consideration: Hedgerows

Although they are hard-working landscape features with an essential ecological function, hedgerows are underused in American gardens. The British countryside, though, is crisscrossed with them, its roads lined with these dense thickets of shrubs and trees that need little or no pruning and provide food and shelter for wildlife. Such living walls can be as useful in gardens as in fields and natural areas, for it is in our denuded cities and suburbs that songbirds, raptors, bees and other insects, and small mammals most need places to hide, sleep, nest, burrow, and feed. Because hedgerows are traditionally composed of mostly deciduous native plants, they take little or no maintenance once they're established. If you choose plants that naturally grow to the size and shape that fit the specific location, then you can let a hedgerow ramble, twine, and weave together without any help from you.

Though evergreen hedging is relatively unchanging in color and texture, hedgerows are a celebration of seasonality, for they leaf out in springtime, bloom, and drop their foliage in autumn. Even in winter, when the deciduous trees and shrubs that make up hedgerows lose their leaves, they remain thick enough to form a visual barrier and an impenetrable boundary. Wild rose hips and the red and yellow twigs of shrubby dogwood (*Cornus sericea* and *C. sericea* 'Flaviramea') provide color through the winter.

We often think of hedgerows as big, thick walls 10 to 15 feet wide, but they can consist of shorter-growing shrubs, or can be planted more narrowly for smaller lots. Most of us have areas of our gardens that are intensely cultivated—usually in front of, or close to the house—that take up most of our gardening attention. We often have side yards or back boundaries where we'd prefer not to spend so much time or money. These are perfect areas to plant in hedgerows that attract birds, bees, and butterflies.

If hedges are all about dividing up space, then mazes must be their quintessential form, made to intrigue and confuse those brave enough to enter into their mind-bending turns and twists.

LEFT: *Slender tree stumps painted vivid red have visual impact far beyond the small amount of space they take up.*

BELOW: *The dramatic splay of giant fennel, a couple of pots, and a slight change of elevation are enough to differentiate one garden space from the next.*

BOTTOM: *A chartreuse picket fence and collection of tin pails and tubs lend enough character to give this space more the feel of an outdoor room than a storage area.*

RIGHT: *A simple wooden moon-viewing pavilion on the shores of a pond is the perfect spot for sipping tea or sleeping outdoors.*

NEXT PAGE: *The destination pattern creates specific places for certain purposes, like this paved and walled outdoor room complete with warm fire and comfy chairs.*

chapter six

DESTINATION

GARDEN DESTINATIONS:

PATTERNS FOR PATIOS, SHEDS, AND FOCAL POINTS

I SPENT MANY HAPPY HOURS one winter thumbing through garden design books, scheming and dreaming about renovating what was then my decade-old garden. I learned plenty about hardscaping, plant selection, hedging, and where to put the garbage cans. But it wasn't the details, elevations, or materials I was interested in; what I longed to create was a garden rich in an atmosphere of invitation and relaxation. I wanted a garden that oozed pleasure, coaxed with its fragrances and flowers, and most of all, offered cozy and comfortable destinations in which

A carved stone column wound with wisteria centers this outdoor dining room destination.

to pause and take it all in. I wanted a garden to inhabit, not just to look at, and it was the patterns of destination that were missing in my plant-centered garden.

The way a garden is experienced doesn't depend on the width of a border or the height of an arbor. It is the atmosphere, the emotional experience, an individual's comfort and response that make a garden memorable. You know how in every recipe there are certain elements vital to the success of what you're making? You can play around with the amount of cinnamon, or even substitute one egg for two when you make gingerbread, but if you leave out the molasses or the baking soda (let alone the flour and sugar) you've got a mess. The essential elements in a "recipe" for planning a new garden, or rejuvenating an older one, might well be enticing destinations.

When I think about the gardens I've enjoyed the most, they all have specific elements in common, such as cushioned benches, gracious dining areas, patterns of shade and sun, and pathways that beckon. It's important to keep these patterns firmly in mind while planning a garden that will work its magic on guest and gardener alike. Gardeners need all the excuses they can find to look up from digging in the soil long enough to enjoy a leisurely stroll to the shed for a sharper shovel, take a morning cup of coffee out to a pondside bench, or linger over dinner beneath the stars. Such a lived-in garden is always recognizable, not only because of the worn spots on the chair cushions, but mostly for its air of comfortable and welcoming repose.

Perhaps the most important point in siting any garden destination is that each space, plant, or vignette needs to suit the topography or situation in which you put it. A tiny patio can be nestled in foliage for privacy, set beneath a

pergola for shade, or placed at the top of a hillside to afford a view out to mountains, water, or the rest of the garden. But there always needs to be a reason to go there, and this you can create with screens, plantings, and furnishings. Planning destinations is somewhat similar to planning garden rooms, but is more flexible, varied, and informal. Think of the destination pattern as creating specific places for certain purposes.

A common mistake is to have all the sitting and dining areas grouped around the house, the garden shed in clear view from the back door, the showiest plants visible from just inside the garden gate. Such visual grouping, however practical, makes a garden not much more than something

BELOW: *In milder climates, outdoor living rooms are destinations that coax you into the open air year-round, complete with cushioned furniture and art on the walls.*

RIGHT: *A stone bench echoes the native material (like the boulder behind the border), providing a place to relax and be enveloped in this plant-rich garden.*

MAKE A GARDEN DESTINATION WORTH THE TRIP

Anticipation makes every journey memorable. Can you think of anything more coaxing to the feet and heart than a narrow curving path mown through a tall, hazy field of grass? You can encourage enthusiasm for the journey by trying some of these ideas to engage the senses and imagination:

• Encourage exploration. No matter whether your garden is flat or small, you can create excitement and tension with plantings (and structures) if you build and plant to obscure rather than to reveal.

• Line a pathway with mounds of textural ornamental grasses or fragrant dwarf lavender shrubs.

• Plain stone or concrete pavers can be interspersed with a mosaic stepping-stone or two.

• Flowery incidents staged along a pathway slow progress. Who can walk by a rose without taking a sniff, or pass a stand of mottled and hooded cobra lilies without stooping to take a closer look at such sinister exoticism?

• Little low-voltage lights outlining the path, or a couple of trees pruned to meet overhead, will enrich the experience while subtly guiding a visitor along the chosen route.

Be sure to make your destinations plant-rich, for leafiness, changeability, and perfume provide the dose of sensuality that makes any garden destination worth visiting often. Fragrance encourages lingering and relaxation; pots of heliotrope, scented-leaf geraniums, or nicotiana waft sweet perfume for months. Or plant a stand of Oriental lilies nearby for a dose of midsummer fragrance.

Plants can be used to break up space or add a little privacy. Lace a vine through a nearby lattice or pergola, or plant up a big pot of rustling bamboo.

An underused corner of the garden can be transformed into an oft-visited destination with a little paving, chairs, and a fire pit.

to look at. Why bother to walk out into the garden when you can step just outside the back door and see everything there is to see? We're beckoned into the depths of a garden by a carefully orchestrated series of destination patterns. In the best gardens it feels as though we have come across such destinations by chance, discovering a patio tucked into a sunny corner, a garden shed with its own little shady terrace, or perhaps a primrose-lined hydrangea walk squeezed into the north-side garden. Sequencing spaces, light, and places to sit, relax, or view art creates a garden that we move through purposefully and joyously in the hopes of discovering such delights.

PATTERN 8: PATIOS

Paved patios and terraces are most often used to tie a house to the landscape, to extend hard surfaces out into the garden. A sunny little patio just outside the kitchen door tempts you to step outside for morning coffee, and a dining terrace close to the house encourages al fresco meals. Though it makes sense to site a sturdy dining table on a patio or deck nearest the kitchen so you'll set it beautifully and use it often, why not install low-voltage lighting along a pathway leading to an underused part of the garden and create a destination there? A private dining or lounging patio featuring a pillow-bedecked bench and a little table for books and snacks, somewhere out in the farthest reaches of the garden, doesn't take much space. If

there's room for a fire pit, a chimenea, or even an overhead heat lamp nearby, this area will quickly become a place to roast marshmallows, drink a glass of wine, lounge around, and enjoy the stars. Because it's easiest to kick back at the end of the day, and we entertain friends most often in the evening, such a corner may well become the most used part of the garden. During the day, the gardener, beset by all the weeding and watering, is hard pressed to take time for a break. If such a space isn't made available and inviting, such respite surely won't happen. Setting the stage with such spaces encourages a gardener to occasionally enjoy the hospitality of his or her own garden. The ideal of developing a habit-forming spot for a visit with friends, or an iced-tea break on a hot afternoon, is furthered by the creation of an area that cries out to be used for such civilized and civilizing pursuits. And while it's not as convenient as a patio or deck right off the kitchen, a walk to a

ABOVE: *This artfully designed little terrace sits behind an Asian-inspired guesthouse on a large rural property, its intimate sense of scale reinforced by the fluffy surround of dwarf fountain grass.*

RIGHT: *A wild patio furnished with doll-scaled metal table and chairs gives a forgotten, Alice-in-Wonderland feel to this corner of the garden.*

more remote area of the garden more than pays off in distance from the telephone, e-mail, and laundry waiting to be folded.

Comfortable and inviting furnishings are a sure way to make your destination patio or terrace worth the trip. Outdoor seating needs to be easeful and commodious as well as durable. Cushions covered with waterproof Sunbrella fabric weather the elements while looking and feeling as pretty and soft as those on an indoor sofa. With all the bulletproof fabrics available, there's no excuse for wooden or metal furniture not to be brightened and made

cushiony with plenty of pillows. Footstools encourage you to put your feet up and stay awhile. Side tables handy for a book, magazine, or drink are every bit as important outdoors as in, and the addition of a little fireplace or heat lamp extends the hours in a day and the months of a year that a patio can be comfortably occupied.

There are several things to keep in mind when you're planning destination patios or terraces. First, the style of the elements you use should be in keeping with the rest of the house and garden in both scale and material. The shade cast by a twig arbor in a rustic, rural garden will be just as cool and pleasurable to sit beneath as that lent by an ornate iron one in a more formal space, or a sleekly burnished pergola in an Italianate setting. Try to be consistent in the scale of paving, furniture, and structures. Although materials don't need to match, and quite often are more interesting if they don't, they should have an affinity with each other. And remember that the surface underfoot doesn't need to be solid. A patio made of pavers interspersed with grass or groundcovers, or a gravel terrace, offers earth-friendly permeability as well as the appeal of a softer surface.

Nestled into a tree at the back of a terrace, this decorative potting bench becomes a place to serve food and drinks at parties, yet is still handy for its utilitarian purpose of potting up.

A garden shed can be the heart of the garden, lending scale, backdrop, and structure, while keeping tools close at hand.

Try to create sitting areas with various patterns of shade and sun, depending upon your climate and preference. Emerging into sunlight at the end of a woodland walk calls out for a bench to sit on and soak up the warmth. Nothing is more welcome in a hot, sunny garden than a chair or two placed in the dappled shade of a tree to escape the glare, or a shadowy seating nook half-hidden beneath a heavily vined arbor.

PATTERN 9: SHEDS

Even a simple garden shed or other work area can be made into a magnetic destination with stepping-stones leading up to its doors, perhaps its own little gate, and a couple of flowery window boxes. Who cares if the shed is filled with twine, shovels, and spades if the approach creates a bit of nostalgia or anticipation? Whether large and well appointed, or just roomy enough to get the wheelbarrow out of the rain, a shed adds height, solidity, color, and texture to a garden. Its location and exterior should be as carefully considered as the delights of its interior—for few garden destinations please a gardener more than a snug, dry shed in which to store seed packets, neatly arranged tools, and bags of soil.

Sheds, potting benches, and other utilitarian garden destinations are perfect opportunities for using recycled materials. A sheet of old metal can be used as a roof; old barnwood adds character; the tines of a rake make perfect hooks on which to hang implements. With some creative

Whether anyone ever sits on it or not, this bench serves the visual function of focal point and underscores the wild, open character of the meadow.

second use of materials, you can save money, as well as insert a little age, character, and interest into the garden.

A clever gardener I know had a path leading to the compost pile in the back corner of her fenced garden. To make following that path more exciting than just another trip to the compost bin, she created a series of incidents along the way, from an urn planted with shiny tufts of ruby and cerise chard to a peeling old paned window hanging by chains from a tree branch. No one who ventures to the back corner is disappointed to find a compost pile, for there are a variety of small set pieces along the way for enjoyment.

PATTERN 10: FOCAL POINTS

A destination need not be as practical as a place to sit; sometimes it's simply a visual lure. While we often site a piece of sculpture or a particularly pretty tree to be viewed from the windows of the house, some of the impact is lost when we see the object so clearly and so often. Creating a setting out in the garden to shelter a statue, frame a fountain, or place an extravagantly planted pot can make each more special, as they aren't so immediately available to us. Also, when we do come upon them, it is a more private experience, so we're more likely to pause and soak in the beauty of a mirror, pond, plaque, or pot.

Destinations can be plantings as well as structures or objects, and in fact for many of us there's no better reason to wander a garden than to check out what's in bloom, finger a leaf, smell a flower, or stroke a tree trunk. A pattern as simple as laying stepping-stones through a border encourages walking through the shrubbery to see it up close. It is discouraging to look at a garden that appears nearly impenetrable in its lushness. By making a garden permeable, with pathways, steps, and sightlines through the plantings, you stimulate people to make their way through the garden rather than just look at it.

The pattern of using plants as focal points, rather than merely creating pleasing plant combinations, is vital to creating garden destinations. For example, when you surround a tree trunk with shrubs and perennials, no matter how carefully they are chosen to go with the tree in texture and color, you create a pattern of flow, perhaps, and naturalism, but not a garden destination. But if you choose a tree with spectacular foliage, such as a *Cercis canadensis* 'Forest Pansy' with heart-shaped leaves in deep plum-red, or an *Acer griseum* (paperbark maple) with cinnamon-colored peeling bark, the tree deserves to be showcased rather than half-buried in plantings. Or several trees, such as

The little grove of birches is grounded by a tall urn, its similar texture and pale color drawing your attention to the trees' beautiful bark.

white-trunked birches or pink-berried mountain ash (*Sorbus hupehensis* 'Pink Pagoda'), can be grouped into a small grove sure to draw you in to stand among them. This pattern of plants-as-destination can be created on any scale, from a pot of bright spring tulips to a towering evergreen tree you can't resist leaning up against to absorb its ancient strength.

FAR LEFT: *The hefty proportions of this geranium draped urn create a focal point in this courtyard garden.*

LEFT: *All it takes is a few square feet of ground to fashion an atmospheric destination. This corner of the garden would rarely be visited if not for the little tableau of chairs, table, and umbrella.*

BELOW: *A destination for all seasons: A fully furnished veranda overlooks extravagantly planted gardens and the smooth rectangle of a concrete pool.*

NEXT PAGE: *We know how we feel when entering a space; using replicable patterns helps us to put these human instincts into words. Here, the pattern of water is used both inside and out to blur the boundaries between house and garden.*

chapter seven

WATER

OUR BASIC ELEMENT:

WATER
PATTERNS

WATER IS AN ESSENTIAL PATTERN in any garden, for it fully engages the senses. Perhaps because I grew up in a garden with a creek running through it, I can't imagine a garden without water. One of earth's basic elements, water is at home in any environment. In an arid garden, a still pond or even a small basin filled with water evokes an oasis, harking back to the first gardens of ancient Persia. In a drippy, damp climate, water reflects passing clouds and reminds us that it is nature's vital, life-giving ingredi-

Flowers planted around the base integrate the birdbath into the garden. It holds a cluster of shiny stones magnified and made luminous by just an inch or two of water.

ent. Water enchants, tranquilizes, and attracts not only humans but also a great variety of creatures that enliven the garden. Birds, bees, frogs, butterflies, and dragonflies will come if you build a pond or stream; no other addition to the garden creates an entire ecosystem as quickly as water. Whether a simple bubble fountain running over rocks or an elaborate installation of streams and waterfalls, a water feature adds mystery and music to the garden, while giving us a more complete experience of nature every time we step out the door.

Water has been a vital ingredient in gardens through the centuries because it is by nature endlessly mutable. Even a small amount can have maximum impact, making a water pattern one of the simplest to introduce into a garden of any size or style. Water introduces the patterns of reflection and movement into the garden. As it runs, eddies, or pools at our feet, it connects us with the earth—we look down and in and are captured by its watery depths. Narcissus couldn't help staring at his image reflected in the water, and we too are drawn in to look closely for the flash of fish, the tattoo of raindrops, the ripple of wind playing across the surface.

Life is possible only where there is water, so the earliest civilizations learned to harness, store, and move water through dams and irrigation canals. Those desert-dwelling early gardeners treated water as a precious resource, using it sparingly to grow fruit and vegetables. But they couldn't help questing after beauty any more than we can, and it wasn't long before ornamental gardens grew up around water sources. Scenes found in Egyptian

tomb paintings (ca. 1600 B.C.) show intimate, enclosed gardens with leafy trees, vine arbors, a few flowers, and most often a pond. The earliest three-dimensional depiction of an ornamental garden, excavated from a Theban tomb (ca. 2000 B.C.), is a miniature wooden boxed model, complete with copper-lined fish pond overhung with tiny carvings of fig trees.

Although early gardeners dealt with the challenges of irrigation and growing food in a harsh climate, their creations went far beyond pragmatism, for they were filled with religious, cultural, and symbolic significance. Ponds and waterfalls not only represented the life source in desert climates but were also created for sheer beauty. Penelope Hobhouse in *The Story of Gardening* described the sacred water lily of Upper Egypt: "In early summer the pools of palace and temple gardens would be transformed into a sea of blue and white flowers." Walled retreats with water, shade trees, and flowers appeal to us today every bit as much as they did centuries ago when any green site was considered sacred. Which is just how most of us feel about our gardens, and no more so than when a fountain, pond, or stream, let alone one filled with exotic blue water lilies, is part of the picture.

PATTERN 11: WATER

Whether you dig a little pond, engineer a system of waterways, or take advantage of nearby scenery by drawing it in with visual trickery, a water pattern satisfies, intrigues, and adds richness to any garden experience. The decisive and charming words of Beverley Nichols, a British garden writer and novelist from the middle of the last century,

LEFT: *A circular pond punctuates the green stillness of a woodland garden, its mossy stone and smooth curve emphasizing the naturalism of the scene.*
RIGHT: *Reflective glass balls float in the pond, playing up the buoyancy of the water, as well as the mirrored effects of its smooth surface, and adding contrast to the structure's hard, straight edges.*

linger as perhaps the definitive statement on how vital the inclusion of water is to good garden-making. He writes in *Garden Open Tomorrow* (reissued by Timber Press in 2002): "Not for the first time, and certainly not for the last, I take this opportunity of reminding the reader that every garden must begin with water in some shape or form, even if it is only a pool two feet square sunk into a little concrete terrace. If the reader's retort is 'In that case I haven't got a garden at all because I haven't got any water in it,' my reply is 'Quite. You haven't got a garden.'"

Pattern Consideration: Still Water—Ponds, Basins, and Birdbaths

When you introduce the pattern of a flat, still pond into a garden, you are in a sense choosing to use water as groundcover. This is a fine technique for creating open space, which you can then plant around (and in). After their ini-

tial filling, ponds use less water than lawn grass, requiring only an occasional topping off rather than weekly watering. Pathways, plants, and sitting areas can all be planned around a pond as a focal point. Whether naturalistic or formal, rimmed with plants or rectilinearly edged with brick or stone, a pond glimmers in the light, reflects trees and the sky, and changes color throughout the day, as well as creating an environment for fish and other creatures. A pond located at the lowest point of a garden can also attractively solve runoff and seepage problems.

BELOW: *This man-made pond is almost lake-like, its scale matching the tall trees it reflects as well as the expansive house and acreage that surround it.*

RIGHT: *Water can be an economical choice of groundcover, as in this spacious pond that reflects the sky, clouds, and glittering sunlight adjacent to a handsome old house and its plantings.*

WATER PLANTS

Size your water feature generously so there's plenty of room for planting the margins with moisture-loving plants. Tufts and sprays of plantings not only effectively blend the pond or stream into the garden but also allow the gardener a whole new palette of plants to play with. A combination of different types of plants helps maintain the pond's ecology, since each type has its function. Because water plants can be invasive, and many areas of the country are fighting problems with "escaped" garden plants, be sure to check with your state's Department of Ecology to make sure any water plants you are considering are not on any noxious weed or invasive plant lists for your region.

When planting a pond or stream, try to choose plants from each of four categories:

PLANTS FOR BOGGY MARGINS. The edges of a stream are naturally muddy, and if you extend the liner out a bit when you build a pond, it is simple to create a shallow bog. You'll be amazed at how quickly water-loving plants grow large and lush in such ideal conditions to form the habitat around the water and stabilize its banks. Ornamental rhubarb (*Rheum palmatum*), hostas, callas, ligularias, and ostrich feather fern (*Matteuccia struthiopteris*) are all showy choices.

POTTED PLANTS. Most plants can simply be submerged in their pots, especially if you've built shallower shelves along the edges of your pond. Cannas, *Iris versicolor*, *Iris pseudacorus*, *Carex pendula*, and water lilies (which appear to float on the surface but in fact are planted in soil) thrive growing in pots. Even the smallest pond or container can hold a pot of dwarf papyrus (*Cyperus haspan*).

SUBMERGED OXYGENATORS. Fish and other pond creatures depend upon oxygen in the water, and these plants help provide it. Because they float or root underwater, their stems and leaves lend protection and habitat for fish eggs, tadpoles, and baby fish. Despite the fact that you won't see much of hair grass (*Eleocharis acicularis*) or water crowsfoot (*Ranunculus aquatilis*), they perform a vital function in diffusing oxygen into the water.

FLOATING PLANTS. Roots and all, these plants float unanchored on the surface of the water, creating a tapestry of foliage and flower as well as shading the water to slow down algae buildup. Water hyacinth (*Eichhornia crassipes*) has waxy-looking leaves, and greater bladderwort (*Utricularia vulgaris*) captures and digests little aquatic insects.

Just as in planning a path, it is well to make a pond larger than you first contemplate. Once it's planted, the edges blur to become part of the garden, the water plants grow up, and the watery surface can become largely obscured. The lushness of water plants creates beauty, but also hides the source of it. Many gardeners have complained that their ponds are not large enough for their newfound water gardening enthusiasm—but I've never heard one say they wished for a smaller pond.

The uses of water in the garden are as mutable as the medium itself. Here, water bubbles and drips from an old mill wheel into a crisply edged, thickly planted pond.

Mountain stones and moss encrusted cedar logs, as well as ferns and draping conifers, integrate a man-made stream and series of falls into the landscape.

A water catchment basin can be as simple as an undrilled pot, its watery surface left empty to reflect the sky, or ornamented with bobbing glass balls or floating flowers. An old horse trough half-buried in the garden and planted in water lilies lends a hint of recycled history as well as beauty, while a tall, textured urn or a fat glossy pot filled to the brim with water creates its own ambience. Basins take minutes to care for—all you need do is refill them after the dog laps up a drink, hose them out every once in a while to keep the water fresh, and perhaps feed a fish or two you've introduced to keep down the mosquito larvae.

Birdbaths, whether the depression in a Zenlike dish rock or an elaborate confection of copper, introduce art into the garden as they raise water up closer to eye level. Taller birdbaths provide a safe place for birds to drink and splash above cat pounce, while giving us a chance to watch birds bathe and preen. At whatever level, high or low, even the smallest birdbath glimmers in the sun, introduces a different material and shape into the garden, and provides a focal point to plant around. Picture tufts of black mondo grass (*Ophiopogon planiscapus* 'Nigrescens') or fluffy *Carex* 'Frosty Curls' trimming out the base of a curvaceously stemmed birdbath, or succulents mounded up around a sleek-lined metal one. Dish rocks, however laboriously transported to the site, add a note of mossy naturalism and an air of aged permanence, appearing as if they'd been hunkered into the ground in just that spot since the last Stone Age. Often birdbaths contribute an artistic note to the garden with their sculptural shapes, sheen of metal, or decorative surfaces, but they have an easy affinity in any garden setting because of their clear and familiar purposefulness.

Pattern Consideration: Moving Water— Waterfalls, Streams, and Fountains

The changing surface of running water, its rushing, gurgling, and dripping, is endlessly alluring, for it quickens and brightens the garden. Water motion is most easily introduced into a garden by a fountain, which can be as simple as a line run up a tree to drip down into the garden or as stylized as a cherub pouring water from a tilted pitcher. No matter how highly designed, any fountain is by its nature an illusion because the machinery and hardware are concealed. This sleight of hand makes the water appear to emerge from a source deep in the earth, or at least from the depths of the pond or pot from which it spills or sprays.

A fountain provides the drip or gurgle of water music that drowns out other noises, attracts attention, and allows you to enjoy your garden's water feature even when you can't see it. Fountains are surprisingly effective at obscuring the sounds of traffic or neighborhood noise. It isn't that the water sounds need be loud enough to mask other noise, it is just that your ear prefers to listen to the sound of water, so that is what you hear rather than the teenager's boom box next door or a car revving up a block away. You don't need the rush and roar of a waterfall to achieve the tranquility and intrigue of water music. Even an occasional drip can be heard through an open window or during a stroll through the garden.

Water is an easy way to age and animate a garden. Dripping, cascading, and flowing down a series of concrete ledges, water appears eternal while moisture loving plants grow in quickly.

Streams, watercourses, and waterfalls can be used to artfully bridge changes of levels in the garden, and such topography makes these features appear as natural as possible. A streambed lined in stone, or the rush of water recirculated from a pond below back up to a waterfall, brings the feel of a fish-filled river into even a small-scale garden. Watercourses can also be highly designed, crafted of metal or stone, and tucked into entryways or alongside terraces. No matter what the style, the effect of water movement and noise is the same. Rocks and waterfalls provide the opportunity to play with the sound the water makes as it pours, eddies, falls, and pools. Perhaps the

ultimate public example of water sound is at the Getty Center in Los Angeles, where installation artist Robert

The misty waters of Puget Sound seem to be pulled right into this waterfront garden, for the rock wall and low plantings subtly direct your eye out towards the distant view.

Irwin designed a bowl of a garden with a cascading watercourse, crisscrossed by bridges and paths, as its central feature. By tinkering with the rocks and the slope, Irwin composed quite different water sounds to be heard at each crossing point. The sensation is one of a watery symphony (and sometimes a jazz band) with such distinct

DEER SCARE

A simple, space-efficient water pattern that fits easily into any style of garden is the traditional Japanese *shishi odoshi*, or deer scare. Also called a water hammer, it has been used in gardens for centuries, and was perhaps first devised to scare deer away with its rhythmic click. Used in many types of gardens, from ceremonial Zen spaces to formal courtyards to rural landscapes, it uses the repeated clunk of hollow bamboo onto wood to focus attention on its self-contained watery world of reflection, pattern, stone, and wood.

A deer scare fountain should be carefully scaled to its surroundings, with accommodation for its splash and drip to be absorbed into the garden. It is made of a reservoir, which can be as rustic as a half whiskey barrel or as sleek as a metal basin. Two pieces of hollowed-out bamboo function as the faucet and the hammer, which create the movement and the click. The deer scare fills and empties with a smooth, rhythmic swish and clack, for when the hammer is full of water it drops to hit upon a stone. The edges of the fountain can be piled with smooth black stones or colorful beach rocks, or planted with ornamental grasses or short bamboo.

changes in tone, rhythm, and decibel level that the journey down through the garden is every bit as much auditory as actual.

Pattern Consideration: Borrowed Water

If you're lucky enough to live anywhere within view of a river or body of water, you can take advantage of borrowed scenery and pull the water right into your garden. View corridors and vistas should be kept open for glimpses of water, however distant, for even a glimpse provides the shimmer of sun off the water, the impression of rolling waves or current burbling along. Trees can be pruned to frame the view, arching to focus the eye toward the blue of the water, which can appear so intimate as to become one of the colors in your garden. Chairs can be placed to look between shrubs or over lower plantings and out toward the view. One of the best water-pattern rewards comes when you are able to combine both a big body of water and an intimate one in the same garden. A basin or pond near your feet while you look out toward more distant water is doubly rewarding, enveloping you in the essence of watery contemplation.

FAR LEFT: *Water, stone, and plants have a natural affinity in their contrasting properties and textures, with water as effective in a formal scheme like this one as when used in a more naturalistic setting.*

LEFT: *The formality of hedging and a classic fountain play off the more tousled look of allium, about to burst into willowy purple bloom.*

BELOW: *The glossy sheen on a grouping of unplanted urns enhances the reflective still pond, while the bulkiness of the pots balances out the heavy-looking stone fountain.*

NEXT PAGE: *We can all be artists in our own gardens if we keep our eyes open and respond to what is happening around us. This gardener had fun with the pun of rusty metal chicken forms planted with hens-and-chicks sedum.*

chapter eight

ART

GARDEN ART:

PATTERNS FOR ORNAMENTATION AND CONTAINERS

ART IN THE GARDEN allows for unrestricted creativity. Perhaps this is because a garden itself is a perfect backdrop for our visions, ideas, originality. Whether garden art is a monumental sculpture or a simple saucer of beach stones, there are few expectations, no roof, no walls, and endlessly changeable lighting. Our own notion of beauty is the only barometer of "correctness." The value or effectiveness of outdoor art lies not in its materials, grandeur, or worth, but in how, where, and with what it is placed.

You could have no better partner in art than nature. The curtain drops as dark falls; dramatic lighting transforms; seasons come and go, bringing with them a varied tapestry of props. Burgeoning foliage and flowers, changing leaves, wind and drizzle, fresh vegetables, winter snow—all change how we see, smell, and feel the garden on any day, or even in any given hour or minute. All the rhythms and cycles of nature, contained in our own gardens, inspire fresh ideas.

Combine nature's unpredictable splendor and ferocity with freedom from expectations and requirements, and the stage is set for an explosion of creativity.

Art objects and containers can be the constant, still points in the garden, with plants growing up and declining,

Recycled gutters and drainpipes find new life as a quirky metal fence, with a short piece of old gutter serving as vase for a "bouquet" of branches.

weather and seasons changing all around them. Or, like glass balls skittering across the surface of a pond in the wind, art can be as mutable as the garden itself. The only real requirement is weather resistance, but that can be gotten around, too, for it's usually possible to shelter pieces inside for part of the year. More easily than art housed indoors, art outside can be incorporated into the very fabric of its setting, as are ornamented fences or mosaic pavers. Or art can equal function: container plantings of fruit or vegetables, birdbaths, birdhouses, fanciful railings, or weather vanes.

PATTERN 12: ORNAMENTATION

Too often, art is added after a garden is complete, as a finishing touch. While art is certainly decorative, to use it only as embellishment or as an afterthought is to miss an opportunity. Garden rooms, boundaries, and plantings can be shaped around art or objects you already own; paving can be poured or laid to incorporate mosaics or found pieces; functional items like weather gauges and even utility sheds can be crafted with style and imagination. At its best, art is integral to the mood and form of the garden.

The material used in art pieces, such as curlicued rusted metal or the gilt that frames a mirror, can itself add artistry to the garden scene. A little garden house can be fitted with stained glass windows, fence posts can be crafted of old garden tools, or a patio can be paved in patterns of pebbles laid on end. Paths can be inlaid with beach stones or shiny river cobbles, and fences or walls can hold niches of meaningful and pretty found objects. I've seen tiny pathway lights made of clear, blown-glass human torsos, hundreds of bowling balls piled up into a pyramid, an overhead arbor decked out in a shimmery chandelier made of purple glass teacups to match the clematis blooming nearby. Think of every surface, underfoot or overhead, as a possibility for color, art, and originality, and your garden will be exciting in all seasons.

Pattern Consideration: Color

"There are chemists who spend their whole lives trying to find out what's in a lump of sugar. I want to know one thing. What is color?"

—PABLO PICASSO

Never underestimate the impact of color. While it is usually what we notice first and remember most, color's influence is far more than visual. Color hits us at a deeper level than merely visual, for it stirs the emotions and tugs at the memory as surely as the smell of hot apple pie spiked with cinnamon or a freshly brewed cup of coffee. I admire a superb colorist more than any other artist, for new color combinations never fail to delight, intrigue, and satisfy me, and cause me to wonder how in the world they figured it out.

Though color is the single most important element in any piece of garden art, it's the most changeable and subjective as well. The season, the light, mood, and memory all affect how we feel about color. Sun, clouds, time of day, moisture in the air or on the piece itself, what is in bloom next to it—all alter how a color looks at any moment.

Think of a garden column painted a pretty pale lilac and encircled with a clematis that blooms magenta in summer. In early spring, when sunlight is weak at best, the column will look refreshingly bright. If a chartreuse grass grows at its base, the lilac color will appear clear and more vivid in contrast. On a stormy day, the column will darken to a muddy violet. In the harsh sun of midsummer, our lilac column will look washy and faded out, and we'll wonder why we even bothered to paint it at all. Then when the intensely magenta clematis bursts into bloom, we'll know that we picked a perfect pastel to sparkle richly as a backdrop. If Picasso pondered the nature of color indoors, he should have tried to figure it out in the garden, where the mystery only deepens.

Color in garden art can be used to warm the garden up, to cool it down, to make a piece appear distant or closer up. One of the most effective ways to use color in

Nature's colors serve architectural elements well; the owner of this bungalow created a little drama by painting her porch steps and railing to match the varied tones of her lacecap hydrangea.

the garden is to play up flower and foliage color, or to substitute for it in the off-season. A fence at the back of the border painted dark delphinium blue will show off the pale blues of springtime, make the yellows of summer appear hotter and richer, and stand in for tall delphiniums themselves during the eleven months of the year when they aren't in bloom. Color can play up style, too: When stucco walls in a shade of saturated mustard are added to the garden scene, any whiff of the Southwestern will be magnified. Natural colors and textures are ideal for Asian-style homes and gardens. Forest greens and brick reds speak of tradition, while shiny galvanized metal, searing blue, and vivid chartreuse hint at modernity. Warm grays, rich black, bronze, and honeyed beiges provide a sheen of sophistication.

When choosing art for outdoors, don't overlook the obvious effectiveness of natural colors and textures. Objects born of wind and weather have an affinity for each other. Stones, shells, and weathered wood mellow the garden and transcend style. Stumps can be left as vertical

accents, stones can be encouraged to grow moss, and smooth boulders set by tree trunks emphasize the roughness of the bark. Natural elements don't fight for attention, but blend harmoniously with other garden elements to create a serenity that enhances the garden experience.

Pattern Consideration: Personal and Salvaged Objects

Our gardens can be as revealing as our fingerprints, telling the story of our own individual pasts, priorities, and aesthetics. And garden art is often the element most expressive of personality in the garden. Well chosen and placed, pieces of art can become the garden's heart and soul, the human spirit of the place. It is surprising how often this is in inverse proportion to expense, size, or grandeur, and more often related to a piece's patina, history, and emotional connections. Whether teacups broken up and used to edge a garden bed, or a wavy antique mirror mounted on the fence to reflect a special view or vignette, pieces with a past lend a sense of storytelling, curiosity, humor, age, and focus to a garden.

Elements that tell a story or infuse a garden with spirit needn't have had a prior life. A new sculpture, birdhouse, or basin, or even a shiny metal pot, will age soon enough when subject to the weather. It is just that recycled and salvaged items are intriguing and eye-catching because they are used in a fresh way the second time around. The inspiration that dawns when you plant moss on the seat of a tired wooden chair, or delineate a flower bed with a rusty old bedstead, seems to leave a residue of welcome, warmth, and individuality. A paint-splattered old ladder can be leaned against the garage to hold a collection of potted plants, and an old push mower can have a second life as sculpture when retired to the vegetable or flower garden rather than to the junk heap.

One way to go about infusing your garden with such spirit is to start collecting objects like old rakes, croquet mallets, watering cans, bowling balls, or whirligigs, and you'll no doubt figure out ways to use them in the garden. Or you can collect objects by shape or material. Rusty metal of varying sizes and shapes can be combined to support plants or form an idiosyncratic arbor or fence. Collections of spheres or egg shapes are rich in symbolism, denoting fertility, infinity, the cosmos. For maximum impact, create loose collages in the garden by grouping objects, whether piled on the ground, hung against a fence

LEFT: *A sculpture that's a tribute to the impact and humor of found objects, this 600-pound iron buoy, dragged home from the beach, sits atop a cylinder of corrugated metal. At night, green lights illuminate the "Daily Planet" sign.*

RIGHT: *A display of lovely old bone china collected over the years at garage sales and flea markets decorates one wall of a garden shed, its flowery patterns echoed in the cottage plantings around it.*

or wall, or integrated into the garden's structure; many found objects look best in juxtaposition with each other.

Another source of inspiration for garden art is to look closely at items you love to determine whether they can stand up to outdoor conditions. There may be a number of objects in your house that could find fresh life outside. When beloved objects find their way into our gardens, the gardens feel like sanctuaries for humans as well as plants and creatures. From groupings of lanterns and candles to dishes filled with agates, shells, or smooth stones, an assemblage in the garden can take on the feel of a personal shrine, an enrichment of the garden experience. A wise artist once said that we all too often ignore how precious plants are, and overemphasize the preciousness of objects. An attitude adjustment might have us placing lovely glass pieces in the garden, and giving special nurture to the plants that surround them.

Pattern Consideration: Inspiration, or How to Be Artists in Our Own Gardens

Art is all about inspiration. Where do we find it? British environmental artist Andy Goldsworthy, who sculpts snowballs in summer, is the ultimate example of collaborating with nature's transience. He celebrates the wind, weather, water, and shaggy cattle that destroy his work, be it twiggy beehives, laced-together leaves, or piles of driftwood lapped away by the next incoming tide. It's all part of the process. This spur-of-the-moment, mutable, unfinished, temporary quality of outdoor art is a great part of its charm, and a never-ending inspiration to garden artists.

All of us who own a garden have access to elements similar to those used by Goldsworthy, right outside our own back doors. Humble and elemental materials like stones, sticks, petals, snow, ice, and leaves are the very stuff of Goldsworthy's work. He comes to each piece without

preconceived ideas, relying on what nature provides in the minute. Goldsworthy says he feels the energy generated by the natural landscape, and transforms it into art for however short a period of time.

With such an attitude, we can all be artists in our gardens if we keep our eyes open and respond to what is happening around us. Nature supplies not only the materials but also an encouragingly casual atmosphere of plenty and

LEFT: *The mosaic that wallpapers this work-of-art shed is crafted of broken bits of china, mirrors, and teacups. The shed's trim is painted to match the brief flurry of springtime poppy bloom.*

ABOVE: *Shallow metal pots planted in overlapping textures of sedum anchor a stone terrace while introducing a note of humor with their Viking-like horns.*

abandon that frees up artistic expression. To use these familiar materials in new ways is at the core of artistic expression, and it is satisfying as well as freeing. For those of us perhaps not quite as talented as Goldsworthy, the fact that rain and wind, sun, tides, and creatures will surely destroy our efforts fairly soon is as comforting as it is disturbing. If nothing else, a Goldsworthy-esque attitude helps us to break rules and express our passions outdoors. It frees us up to move objects about the garden, lets us take advantage of the changing seasons, and spurs us on to see natural objects in ways we might never have thought of before. In contrast to the more permanent pieces by which we anchor the garden, such transitory works of art are more fleeting than perennial bloom, buds on a branch, or snow melting in the sun.

PATTERN 13: CONTAINERS

Containers allow for great garden artistry along with maximum flexibility. Whether a single window box or a garden full of raised beds, they're the perfect vehicle for personal expression. With containers, we can indulge both plant lust and our desire for ornamentation and elaboration, without lasting repercussion to budget or landscape.

Nothing challenges and improves a gardener's eye for combinations like composing container plantings. Design, proportion, color, and shape are all vital to the orchestration of container vignettes, for they're a microcosm of the garden, its distilled essence stuffed into a single pot. Small enough not to overwhelm with either expense or complexity, containers encourage us to look closely, to consider carefully, and—perhaps most important—to experiment. They hone our visual sense, and what we learn in planting up pots can be translated to the garden on a larger scale. (Or what often happens is that people find container gardening to be so satisfying, fun, and stimulating that they minimize the rest of their garden to concentrate on their potted plantings.)

A container planting can be everything from fluffy layers of mixed bouquets to an austere bonsai where a single curved line is all. From an urn so prized for its sculptural shape that it's left empty, to a glazed pot filled with plants or water, there's a container possibility for nearly every spot in the garden that needs accent, color, substance, or a vertical line. You can plumb a container to turn it into a simple fountain, or simply fill an undrilled pot with water to reflect the sky or float glass balls. Pots are the perfect place to grow plants too flamboyant to blend well in the garden, possible invasives, or plants so new to us we aren't sure yet how they'll develop, as well as plants too tender to make it through the winter. Just looking at a container sparks us to picture what we can put into it.

Containers themselves are decorative elements, whether round, rough stone or elegantly tall and glossy. But even more compelling is that plants look different, and often grow better, when held aloft. Soil mix and watering can be more easily controlled than in the ground, plants can be better protected from slugs and snails, and soil warms up earlier in the spring (it also freezes more quickly so some container plants may need winter protection).

You can move pots about to find a shady spot, or to capture the most sun. I always keep a few favorite pots empty to move into the garden to cover up bare spots in early spring, late in the summer, or after the sweet peas give it up. This is often a better solution than rushing to fill in with plants in the ground, because often you won't want

LEFT: *Placed by themselves, any of these objects would visually melt into the landscape. Small pots look best grouped with other items of like or contrasting textures and colors, such as these beach stones and metal lantern.*

RIGHT: *This cauldron of a metal pot would be an effective focal point at the edge of the woods even if it wasn't planted!*

Matching containers to plantings is an artistic challenge; sedums look their best in smooth and shallow pots that don't distract from their compelling textures and forms.

plants in that spot at other times of the year. If you have heavy garden soil, pots will give you a chance to grow bulbs and silverlings that prefer quick-draining soil. And what an opportunity to soften and add interest to paved areas: just set a pot or two on the porch, deck, balcony, or patio, and you've increased your gardening space exactly where you want it. Pots add verticality to the garden, an effect that can be emphasized by elevating them on a wall, pedestal, or post. When you can see plants at eye level, you're sure to notice characteristics you miss when the plant grows at your feet. A pot holding a weathered pine, a dramatic brugmansia, or a bold phormium is a stand-alone focal point, or you can bring cohesiveness to a variety of treasured plants by grouping them together in similar pots.

Pattern Consideration: Matching Pots to Plantings

Look long and hard at the shape and material of the pot before you choose plantings, for pots create many different auras: solidity, age, elegance, whimsy, classicism, or modernity. They speak of the Mediterranean, England, or the Southwest. Not that you can't play against type by planting an elegant metal urn with a topknot of rainbow chard and lettuces, or a rough brown cube with dozens of exotic-looking parrot tulips. But whether you're planting in harmony or contrast, the pot sets the tone.

You can be a purist and keep all your pots in a similar color, shape, or texture, or you can collect pots that simply appeal to you, whether they're polka-dotted ceramic, metal, or painted wooden troughs. If you're unsure about what pot works best, fat terra-cotta ones are versatile and timeless. If you start with a pot you really love, one that is so fabulous it looks good even when empty, you won't go wrong. With the right container, simple is satisfying—think of copper rounds overflowing with a single kind of scented-leafed geranium, or a yellow water lily floating in an aqua-glazed pot.

I once received a gift of a heavy aggregate pot. I tried to figure out how tall a tree or shrub I should plant to balance out the pot's tall, solid shape. But nothing seemed quite right. Then one day I stepped back a bit, blurred my eyes, and saw the rough texture and curved shape as so dramatic that I didn't want to interfere. So I planted the pot up with a coating of variegated sedums that echoed

Instead of a bouquet of different kinds of flowers stuffed into a single pot, a more modern look is one kind of plant per container, which best shows off an individual plant's characteristics.

the colors in the pot and skimmed its surface, adding a top layer of complementary texture. It was not only the most pleasing of my containers, but the easiest to care for.

Pattern Consideration: Mixed Bouquets vs. One Plant

Sophistication results from restraint, and this effect is most true when you limit yourself to one kind of plant per pot. The common becomes extraordinary when singled out in a container of complementary color and shape. Think cherry tomatoes spilling down the sides of a cobalt-blue urn, a simple round pot stuffed with a single kind of colorful coleus, or a tarnished metal basin filled with sunny nasturtiums. This kind of potting strategy offers maximum flexibility, for pots can be regrouped as plants

TIPS FOR SUCCESSFUL POTTING

In mixed containers, always plant generously. Skimpy pots are pitiful, a wasted chance for beauty. Squeeze in as many little root balls as you possibly can, and you'll be gratified with the look of overflowing abundance.

Think of containers as the necklace, shoes, and earrings of the garden—accessories that make the whole garden ensemble individual and eye-catching. As with jewelry, sometimes when you step back and take a look at the overall effect, it is clear that simplification is needed. With accessories, this critical glance often reveals you need to remove one thing before leaving the house. With containers, perhaps you don't need a plant dangling over the edge, or maybe the verbena needs to be repeated all around the rim instead of sticking out by itself on the side. Or that lovely pink stripe in the canna can carry the color scheme just fine without the distraction of those pink impatiens, or …

Each pot needs to both excite and rest the eye. The key is to establish a dynamic relationship between the plant and the pot, through shape, texture, or color. Picture a burst of spiky dracaena emerging from a smooth, round pot, or tall pastel cottage tulips packed into an earthenware urn. Using just one kind of plant per pot rests the eye, with the excitement generated by the contrast between plants and pot.

Plants in pots must live in just the soil provided, so they are deeply dependent on your care. Start with a good commercial potting soil and add some manure, and perhaps some perlite if the mix seems heavy. Water often, which is usually daily once the weather warms up. In pots tightly packed with plants, rain won't be able to reach and penetrate the soil, so be sure to water on misty, drizzly, and even rainy days. Annuals, which give their all in one season, need to be fertilized at least every couple of weeks with diluted liquid fertilizer.

come in and out of flower, or just as your mood dictates. You can create a stylish mix using a diversity of pots and plants, or you can group similar plants or similar pots together. Raise some of the pots up on pedestals, put others into the background, and each plant is shown off to best advantage.

Containers with mixed plantings can be a little trickier. The softening and soothing effect of foliage is the most effective way to rest the eye, for golden, silver, or chartreuse leaves create harmony between various flowers. The addition of lacy verbena, airy nandina, or a backdrop of purple foliage plants, such as a dark smoke bush or elderberry, can make all the difference between a mixed plant-

Containers in the garden can be art in and of themselves, as in this vase by glass artist Dante Marcioni. Its fragility contrasts with the down-to-earth beauty of leeks, potatoes, and roses.

ing with good energy or not. And make sure the flowers aren't all tiny or all large; varying flower sizes and shapes is a sure way to stir up a little visual stimulation.

Texture is as important as color. Feathery bronze fennel, the fountain shape of ornamental grasses, and frothy artemisia are all effective. Think bold, wispy, lacy, sprawling, vertical, horizontal, spiky, rough, and smooth as much as gold, silver, green, and purple.

When you're mixing plants within a single pot, maybe the only rule to remember is to make sure that each and every plant looks as if it has a reason to be there. Every single plant in the mix needs to relate to its pot-mates. I don't go along, however, with rules such as "Use only three different kinds of plants per pot" or "Repeat colors." The eye can easily pick up much more subtle correlations and repetitions than obvious color echoing. There is nothing more discouraging than a pot planted with marigolds,

THE PERFECT, ALL-PURPOSE NEUTRAL

Charcoal gray shows off all other colors better than any other single color. It's the perfect neutral, with enough substance to stand alone, yet the ability to blend beautifully with shades from pastel through vivid bright, all of which look their best set against dark gray. Charcoal is both warm and cool, deep and soft, and isn't as jarringly contrasty as black. It keeps pastels from looking too sweet, yet sets off hot oranges and reds to perfection. Used as flooring, backdrop, or house color, gray can make the garden really pop to show off a specific piece of art, mosaic, or leafy green.

(Mosaic by Jeff Bale)

pink petunias, and red geraniums. What's the point? Combinations can be concocted to fit varied aesthetics, and for all kinds of reasons (food, fragrance, colorful, avant-garde); just make sure that each component contributes to the purpose, or you end up with goulash. The only other tenet I always stick to, and only because it's so pleasurable, is that some plant in every single pot should be fragrant. It's easy to toss in a lily bulb or two, heliotrope for summer, sweet-smelling narcissus in springtime. And pair those red geraniums with glossy tufts of orange/bronze *Carex testacea* and dark, willowy chocolate cosmos (*Cosmos atrosanguineus*), skirted in chartreuse drifts of fuzzy licorice plant (*Helichrysum petiolare*), for a fragrant and unexpected combination of plantings.

Pattern Consideration: Year-Round Potting

It's possible to create a lasting garden in a large pot by layering plants for different seasons. This can require a leap of conceptualization, since most gardeners start out with containers for annual color. A big, frisky dog started me gardening in pots. My German shepherd could behead a row of tulips with a wag of his tail, and with a single step of his massive paw squish new annuals into mulch. So I began thinking of the garden as divided into two distinct parts: permanent plantings in the ground, more delicate and seasonal plants in pots. But this so limits the possibilities, as well as excluding the fun of pots in seasons other than summer. So now every pot in my garden that's sufficiently large (at least 24 inches across) is planted with bulbs, climbing roses, small trees, shrubs, annuals, perennials—anything I want to feature, protect, look at more closely, or grow in a spot where garden beds don't provide ideal conditions. Often this spot is right outside one of the doors, as with the rosemary that grows year-round in a terra-cotta pot near the kitchen, joined by heat-loving annual herbs in summer. Or the big container near the front door that offers up spring bloom, summer fragrance, and dozens of swooningly sweet-smelling paperwhite narcissus at Christmas.

A simple clay container fashioned like a woman's face and fastened to a telephone pole becomes a neighborhood attraction when filled with seasonal flowers like these poppies and daisies.

For example, a nice big pot on a back patio near an arbor could hold a clematis to wind up the post and bloom overhead in summer. Small-leafed variegated ivies could drip down the side of the pot, and ruffly heucheras in bright chartreuse (*Heuchera* 'Lime Rickey') or warm brown (*H.* 'Chocolate Ruffles') could fluff out the pot. In earliest springtime, crocuses planted near the top of the pot emerge, followed by narcissi planted a little deeper. In July, three fragrant lilies, planted deeper yet, put in a showy, fragrant appearance. Edge with winter-blooming

A found doll's head is an eye-catching addition to a potted arbor arrangement of passion flower vines and willowy Verbena bonariensis.

many years with a little root pruning, freshening of the soil, additions of compost, and regular watering.

Pattern Consideration: Foliage

Whether in year-round pots or those planted up for summer color, foliage plays a dominant role in unifying, electrifying, and carrying the planting for months on end. Coleus and abutilon are color schemes all by themselves. With the luminous chartreuse, warmly auburn, or near-black scalloped leaves of the new heucheras, or the fatly striped paddle-shaped splays of *Canna* 'Tropicana', you won't miss the flowers. But foliage doesn't need to be exotic or colorful to capture attention. Dwarf conifers are pettable plants, and easier to touch and admire when contained, since they're often overlooked and overgrown in a border. Many of these appealing little conifers are variegated or have especially long needles in proportion to their size, plus they live happily for years in pots. And don't overlook interestingly shaped plants, such as the wire netting bush (*Corokia cotoneaster*), which creates a swirl of excitement in a pot, for it appears to always be having a bad hair day. Pots planted exclusively for foliage interest look good over many months. Even when you're planting for flowers, be sure to consider what their own foliage, or the addition of foliage plants, will do for your composition.

Pattern Consideration: Potted Edibles

You can plant an entire vegetable garden in pots or raised beds. Heat-loving vegetables, fruits, and herbs thrive when raised up. These plants tend to sprawl about, so they look their best contained, where the hard edge of a pot or raised bed contrasts with their profusion.

Plant a tomato in a pot on the patio, some ruffly lettuces nearby, and basil in a third pot, and you have texture, color, and salad. Give eggplant (try the startlingly dark-leaved 'Slim Jim') and corn a better chance to ripen by planting in pots, and if you don't get a crop, you'll at least have spectacular foliage to enjoy all summer long.

pansies in autumn, which, along with the heucheras and ivy, will carry the show through the winter until the crocuses emerge again. Or a year-round pot can be centered with a woody plant, like a corkscrew hazel (*Corylus avellana* 'Contorta') or perhaps a colorful little spirea (*Spiraea japonica* 'Magic Carpet'), or a hydrangea if the pot is in the shade, with bulbs planted beneath the roots of the tree or shrub, and perennials or annuals tucked in around the sides. If you think of any kind of plant as a possible subject for container culture, you'll unleash the creativity to see plants in new ways. Most plants can be kept in pots for

MOSAICS

Mosaics are perfect for creating inspired color combinations in the garden. An art of bits and pieces, they are pleasingly intricate, inviting you in for a closer look. Mementos such as old watches, cups, jewelry, or coins can be embedded into them as visual history, a durable garden scrapbook. Mosaics are equally effective whether made up of the subtle tones and textures of pebbles laid on their sides—an art both ancient and current—or shiny, bright fragments of broken mirrors or ceramic bits. The vivid liveliness of mosaics holds its own in the most overplanted gardens, and coaxes us outdoors during the brown, bleak times of the year. How many art forms hold up in rain and freezing cold and fit easily into the hardscape of a garden? Whether used in garden construction as walls around ponds, in tiled fountains and pavers, or as the material of birdhouses, birdbaths, pots, or mirror frames, mosaics offer a chance for personal expression that fits particularly well into the garden.

(Mosaic by Clare Dohna)

A number of edibles are marketed for growing in containers, such as the compact tomatoes 'Patio' and 'Sweet Baby Girl' that don't grow so wildly huge. Easy to grow from seed, the nonheading cut-and-come-again leaf lettuces are variously colored and ruffled, and all are deliciously tender. Just keep snipping, and the plants keep on producing. Blueberries are handsome plants with great fall color, and hardy dwarfs like 'Polaris' and 'Chippewa' are small enough to live happily in pots for years. Edibles ripen faster when corralled and elevated. Leafy posts of columnar apple trees can form a living railing along the edge of a deck, grown in pots placed 2 feet apart; come

autumn, you could just step out your door and pick an apple. 'Scarlet Sentinel' and 'Golden Sentinel' are both bred for disease resistance and high-quality fruit, and the former stays small enough to grow in a container. 'North

ABOVE: *Sheds lend structure, interest, and destination to the garden. The recycled old windows in this one let in enough light so that tender potted plants can be overwintered through the chillier months of the year.*

RIGHT: *The hard edges and geometric shapes of raised beds organize the tousled look of flowers, vegetables, herbs, and fruits all planted together. Elevated soil warms up earlier in the spring to encourage the edibles; watering, fertilizing, and slug control are all easier in a confined environment.*

ORNAMENTATION FOR SCALE AND DIMENSION

Art, like architecture, is a great tool for manipulating the scale of the garden, so think of using it not only in various sizes, but also at every level of the garden. Nothing is more dull and static than a garden on a single horizontal plane where the interest hovers at ground level, or one where most plants top out at human height, a level at which the mirrors, lamps, and other items of décor also reside. Art affords the opportunity for adding delight, interest, and focal points close to the ground, at eye level, and overhead; distant from the house; or enclosed in a garden room. Using art in this way lends dynamism to the garden in every season, for it keeps you looking up, down, near, and far, as well as wandering through the space to experience the pleasures around every corner.

Besides the intrinsic beauty, humor, or mystery of each distinct piece, art serves an important stabilizing function in the garden. Plants grow, bud, flower, leaf out, die down, and shed their leaves through the seasons, which can significantly alter the garden's focal points, privacy, height, and solidity. This is why gardens are so endlessly interesting. But not all these seasonal changes improve our experience of the garden. Because art doesn't change until you move it or alter it, a tall sculpture or carving can preserve height in a distant corner of the garden in winter when a nearby deciduous tree has lost its impact. A big bronze sphere or a collection of bowling balls can maintain a garden's dimensionality nearer to the ground when plant life is at its skimpiest. In late autumn, when the garden turns drab, a brilliant-toned mosaic piece, or a stucco wall painted azure blue or persimmon orange, can warm and spark the garden until spring color returns.

A leafy tree, or even a large shrub, can link house and garden and blur the lines between indoors and out in spring and summer. But in the colder months of the year, when its branches are bare, the lines of demarcation between vertical and horizontal planes may look too severe. Large pieces of statuary or even tall containers can serve this softening and linking function year-round. Smaller pieces, like urns, mirrors, gargoyles, and birdbaths, can link the house to the garden stylistically—whether the style be formal, funky, Arts and Crafts, or Asian—or through affinity of color, texture, or materials.

Pole' is a variety with large red juicy apples similar to a McIntosh. Raised beds or large containers organize edible plants, as well as make it easier to provide good soil, adequate water, and nutrients.

Lee Kelly's garden is populated by the silent, timeless presence of his huge metal sculptures. He says the artwork is the human presence in the garden, the spirit of the place.

FAR LEFT: *This garden owner plays with scale, grouping an outsized statue with a vase and metal pergola to give his tiny urban garden a sense of place.*

LEFT: *Containers deserve a second look when they're a mix of the familiar, like these nasturtium leaves, with more exotic species, like carnivorous pitcher plants (*Sarracenia flava*) that trap insects in their throat and drown them in a toxic nectar.*

BELOW LEFT: *Pebble mosaics introduce intricate, colorful patterning underfoot—and the promise of a reflexology treatment if smooth stones are used in the construction.*

BELOW RIGHT: *The most arresting garden art uses familiar objects in new ways; here, a deck finial is crafted from shards of wire-wrapped beach glass stuck in a flower pot.*

NEXT PAGE: *Whether your garden is tiny or expansive, thinking in patterns allows you to play with spaces and materials. This vignette is effective because the floppy foliage and rough wood backdrop contrast with the oval shape and glossy paleness of the little bonsai pot planted with sedums.*

chapter nine

SHAPE

SHAPING THE GARDEN:

MATERIAL
PATTERNS

WHEN WE START OUT TO MAKE A GARDEN, what we're really doing is covering the ground, as well as building outdoor walls and roofs. We create the very fabric of the garden with our material choices. Whatever we walk on, walk beneath, or lean against has color, texture, finish, and heft. The look and substance of garden materials either reinforces the garden's atmosphere or detracts from it. Although we first notice color or texture when we choose pavers, stone, or wood for the garden, it's easy to overlook some more vital characteristics of materials.

Granite pavers laid in a spiral shape create a swirling vortex, drawing us down into the comfort of the cushioned chaise. The dark, lacy leaves of the Japanese maples create a pleasing contrast to the rough, pale pavers.

PATTERN 14: MATERIALS

When people update their gardens, they usually cut down on lawn size to save time and resources. Often they leave a small patch of grass, explaining that it's for the children or the dog. I think we sense the need for this soft, tactile surface in contrast to paving, and leave it for ourselves every bit as much as for the dog. There are other ways besides lawn to cover the ground with something besides hard surface, but grass is the most familiar to us. A large expanse of pond to reflect the sky, gravel, mounds of groundcover, raked sand, wood decking, and raised beds all lend softer textures and visual interest.

We need to pay attention to each material's bulk, solidity, heft, and softness, as well as its light-reflecting quality, for these are the attributes that read most clearly in the garden. Surface patterning and color should really be among our last considerations when we are choosing materials. Whether a garden feels sturdy, solid, and safe, whether there are soft surfaces mixed with hard ones, and how the light is absorbed by surfaces or reflected off them—all affect our felt sense of the garden at its most basic level.

Pattern Consideration: Light Absorption and Reflection

What happens when light strikes various garden materials greatly alters the mood, feel, and temperature of the garden. Green leafy plants absorb light; they actually draw it in and make use of it to produce chlorophyll. In contrast, the man-made and hardscape elements are the parts of the garden easily alterable to influence light's resonance in the garden.

The effect light has greatly depends on your climate, and varies through the seasons. In winter, when the sun slants low, it hits the garden very differently than when its arc is high overhead for many hours of the day. In the Northwest, where skies are overcast so much of the time, gardeners want to take advantage of every possible drop of sunlight. Expanses of still water, light colors, gold-toned plants, and reflective surfaces all magnify light. In sunnier, hotter climates, it isn't only shade that cools the garden, but matte, light-absorbing surfaces and cooler colors.

BELOW: *Large slabs of stone are laid so that tufts of ornamental grasses lap at their corners, softening hard edges yet retaining the open expanse of stone.*
RIGHT: *A masterful mix of materials creates a charming outdoor shower, with painted door, shake siding, pavers underfoot, and shelter overhead.*

Whenever you choose a material, be sure to consider how shiny or reflective it is. A stucco wall painted a deep pine green will absorb light, creating a shadowy effect. If you place a mirror on the wall, it'll appear to be a bright, shiny window, its reflective qualities heightened by the dark absorption around it.

When I was visiting a retirement community near Phoenix, Arizona, I was surprised at the austerity of the plantings, and at how much pale, glittery lava rock and light-colored paving dominated the landscape. The groundscape offered no respite from the sun—rather, it multiplied the heat, for the sun bounced off the ground in shimmering waves. When I drove a few miles down the road to Taliesin West, Frank Lloyd Wright's former winter residence now open to the public, it was a relief just to walk through the gates. Here there were plenty of green plants, vines covering the walls, and a mix of surface textures and colors to absorb some of that sunshine. I looked up to see whether the sky had clouded over, so dramatic was the change; it felt at least ten degrees cooler, and the sun's glare far less intense. But the sky was just as blue and the sun just

as bright. At ground level, though, there was something to absorb all that energy instead of amplifying it.

Pattern Consideration: Materials Underfoot, Overhead, and In Between

Our garden experience is informed by what's underfoot, whether we ever look down or just take it for granted that we'll find solid, secure footing. Our tactile sense is affected, as we feel the ground beneath us give way a bit, or sense that it's uneven or hard, cold or warm, smooth or rough.

Overhead elements, often referred to collectively as the built canopy, need to relate to the architecture of the house in scale and material. If an arbor or pergola can be tied in to the roof of the house, extend out from a garage, or shel-

ABOVE: *Passing through this garden is a textural adventure! Imagine how sterile it would feel to walk along a wide, paved pathway without the tumble of plants, rather than to pick your way along these pavers.*

RIGHT: *A smooth board fence, mossy bricks underfoot, and concrete retaining walls create a warm, sheltered patio for growing edibles and flowers. The metal furniture and terra-cotta pot on the table complete the inspired mix of materials.*

ENVIRONMENTALLY FRIENDLY MATERIALS

It makes sense to construct a living organism like a garden out of "green" materials. Where better to show our respect for nature than in our own gardens? Look for materials that are nontoxic, recycled, reused, local, and resource-efficient. Quality matters, for durable materials with a long life cycle don't need to be replaced as often. As you plan your garden, remember that using fewer materials and just less of everything may be the ultimate statement in green style.

Here are some ideas and products to consider:

Pre-used materials like old doors, windows, cobbles, glass, bricks, and metal are less expensive than new ones, and their patina adds age and layers of interest to a garden.

Give your garden its own "backstory" by using broken-up bits of china to edge beds, creating a fountain out of galvanized metal pipe, or roofing an arbor with an old satellite dish planted with moss and ferns. I've seen cylindrical concrete catch basins used as hunky retaining walls and planters, and cast-iron welding tables out of an old shipyard put to new use as sturdy porches. Old objects used in new ways showcase creativity while saving money and the earth.

Biopavers are interlocking concrete pavers that integrate plants and impervious surfaces. The plants are manufactured right into the paver, and after installation are "unwrapped" through biodegradation. Biopavers come with prepacked soil and plants as part of the package. The plants soften the look and feel of the concrete while filtering contaminants from storm water as it passes through the paver. (www.biopaver.com)

Green roofs absorb rainwater, reduce energy use, last longer than composition, and look great. They also form a wildlife corridor in the sky, offering save haven, food, and shelter for birds and insects. A green roof is simply a layered sandwich of roof deck, waterproof membrane, and soil filter fabric, topped off with several inches of soil mix and plants. A residential-quality living roof can be built for eight to twelve dollars per square foot, about the same price as tile or slate, about twice as much as metal. (www.greenroofs.net)

Other environmentally sensitive products:

- Recycled lumber. Avoid treated lumber; it leaches chemicals into the soil.
- Recycled glass chips.
- Bamboo fencing.
- Pavers made of old tires and other rubber products.
- Planters and outdoor furniture made of recycled milk jugs. (www.orcaboard.com)
- Trex is a wood substitute made of reclaimed wood and plastic. Sturdy, long-lasting, and maintenance-free, it can be used for decking, railing, and benches, and to edge raised beds. (www.trex.com)

ter a gate, so much the better. The material, color, and style of the house itself should set the tone. A weathered cedar arbor might look best with a shingled house, while a stucco cottage would be enhanced by brightly painted fencing or furniture. Utility and scale must come first in choosing materials, and the simpler and stronger the better, for these elements provide an experience of shelter and shade first, and a decorative element second. Any sense of flimsiness, a rickety or leaning post, or a lack of connection between an overhead element and its supports immediately makes you feel nervous and unsure. For any overhead structure, don't even consider ready-made trellising, or any material without the bulk to support a full-grown wisteria vine. Even if you have no intention of planting any vine at all on your structure, keep a wisteria trunk in mind as a touchstone for scale.

The liquid look and shimmery pale flow of Japanese forest grass (Hakonechloa macra 'Aureola') is an ideal counterpoint to the geometric shape and hard surface of stone pavers.

The choice of material visually reinforces the bulk and heft of these elements. Simple, rough wood; textural stucco; concrete cylinders—all are reassuringly heavy and solid looking. You want these elements to appear as if they've grown out of the earth like giant sequoias, to signal that their roots go deep and that the shelter they offer is permanent and secure. Even when a porch has a glass roof or skylight, or when a pergola or an arbor is open to the elements, the feeling should be of substance, solidity, and strength.

Although we mostly concentrate on covering the ground or on creating shelter overhead, the materials we use in between—those that rest mostly at eye level—are probably the ones we notice most. This layer of the garden

includes walls, hedges, fencing, raised beds, screens, trellises—the forms that contain and delineate the garden. Mostly these materials take their cue from what is used on the ground, or overhead, and from the house and driveway. The materials they are made of, and the scale of these elements, need to relate more closely to the house than does the paving; while a mix of wood, stone, and concrete adds interest and texture, most of the elements near eye level serve as backdrop for plants, and shouldn't be considered as star players.

If you introduce new materials in this layer that contrast with the house, be sure to repeat them for continuity. For example, galvanized metal screening looks modern, and it's inexpensive, lightweight, and durable, so it's good for screening and fencing. It introduces reflectivity and shininess in this mid-level of the garden, to bounce sunlight off the walls of the garden and give a silvery sheen. But you wouldn't want to have just one patch of such an eye-catching material. Sheets of metal could be framed in wood for a gate in a wooden fence, or a nearby screen or trellis could be built of galvanized hogwire to echo the metal of the screening. Such continuity or echoing of material is especially important at this very visible layer of the garden.

Nevertheless, it's important to explore options at this level of the garden as at all others. When I recently built a new garden, my hardest decision was what material to use for the raised beds, which would range from 1 foot to 4 feet high. I talked with designers, architects, and gardeners in search of an environmentally sound, inexpensive, sturdy solution. I planned to grow vegetables, so treated wood was out, plus I didn't want the chemicals from the wood leaching into my garden. I wasn't interested in the rustic look of cedar, which when planted up almost blends

Expanses of stone or concrete slabs radiate a warm micro-climate where heat-loving plants like these sedum and Mexican daisies (Erigeron karvinskianus) flourish.

in with the plants. I appreciated the solidity and stability of brick, but it looked too traditional for the modern garden I was planning. I considered Trex, a wood-and-polymer product that is durable, colorful, and reasonably inexpensive, but it gets wobbly and lacks integrity when placed on its side, so I didn't feel it would be sturdy enough for the taller raised beds. I was hoping to avoid mortar just because of the extra labor involved, but ended up deciding on split-faced CMU's (concrete masonry units), which did need to be mortared in place. Because these rough concrete blocks now come in 4-inch widths that, when the beds are filled with soil and plants, look as thick and hefty as the typical 8-inch size, they are space-effective and sturdy. I couldn't be more pleased with the result, for the raised beds look nicely utilitarian, and as if they've been in the garden for many years. The tops are capped, so they're wide enough to sit on when gardening or visiting, and the hard, industrial look of the block is a great foil to the profusion of plantings contained in the beds.

STONE. Stone can look rugged, aged, classy, or all three at the same time. Because stone is a natural material, its colors and patterns fit easily into the garden. Stone paving gives even a brand-new garden a feeling of history and permanence. Because stone is both expensive and significant, it can be used effectively yet sparingly in low walls or scattered stepping-stones to age and solidify the garden. Randomly shaped stones lend a casual, cottage effect, while stone cobbles or flagstones suit a more formal scheme. But beware that too much stone, even when the plants have grown in, can feel cold, hard-edged, and even a little daunting or pretentious.

Often stone is shown to best advantage when it is mixed with wood decking, brick, and concrete in similar color tones. Use this most expensive, solid, and showy material where it will be most seen and appreciated, such as in an entry sequence, the main terrace and surrounding low wall, or to pave a dining pavilion. Then the deck and steps outside the kitchen could be built of wood, paths graveled for permeability, and garden areas farther from the house defined with concrete pavers. Such a mix of materials is economical and can feel inspired, while featuring stone to its best advantage.

CONCRETE. Concrete is inexpensive, sturdy, and good-looking, but unfortunately it's all too often formed into ready-made shapes, with finishes that could be more attractive. It looks its best unadorned and in simple, geometric shapes that show it off for what it is without trying to disguise the fact that it's concrete. From rubble walls to aggregate pavers, concrete sets a straightforward and practical tone that suits outdoor spaces and many styles of gardens. It can be poured, in whatever form or texture or color you prefer. It can be colored and stamped to mimic pavers or bricks. It can be mixed with grass in the product Grasscrete, a wafflelike paving strong enough for cars to drive on. Grasscrete gives driveways a texture that's softened by tufts of green, and it's permeable, to prevent runoff.

Though we tend to think of concrete as a uniform bland gray, it can be integrally colored and comes in shades from almost creamy to charcoal. Concrete looks most nearly organic in exposed aggregate, which shows off the various pebble colors for a more natural look. Pavers in varying colors can create interesting contrasts when used in checkerboard patterns of light and dark for a lively, modern effect. Or geometric pavers can be interspersed with duplicate shapes of gravel or grass for contrasting patterning underfoot.

GRAVEL. Gravel gives a hard, dry, durable, and inexpensive surface that allows rain to penetrate and drain through. And it isn't just your plain old gray bits and chunks anymore, but comes in a wide variety of colors, sizes, and shapes. From warm and classy caramel-colored bits of marble to the contemporary, industrial feel of charcoal chunks, gravel can be a style-setter as well as the ulti-

An intersection of the three most familiar of groundcovers (lawn grass, pavers, and gravel) enlivens and varies the experience of the garden journey.

mate practical material. Tiny pea gravel can be raked into swirls or stripes (but beware of how it travels indoors stuck in the soles of your shoes). Whatever the scale, be sure to think about strong edging materials to keep gravel where you want it. Edging of wood adds a warmer feel, while galvanized metal edging looks modern.

Gravel's greatest virtue is also its main drawback. Because gravel isn't a solid surface, cleaning leaves and debris off it can be a chore, as can pulling weeds that sprout up through it. But this permeability also means that gravel can be planted with bulbs and heat-loving plants. Or the gardener can take a less active approach, and allow self-seeders to colonize gravel wherever a softer, flowery look is desirable. Gravel patios are fresh-looking, modern, and practical, for they can bloom with tulips and alliums in springtime, then hold a table and chairs in summer. Gravel pathways and patios can be inlaid with stepping-stones for color and variety, or planted with moss or some other groundcover for softness. In beds and borders, gravel can even be used as a heat-conserving and weed-smothering mulch.

BRICK. While concrete, stone, and gravel are chameleons that suit a variety of styles and eras of gardens, brick always looks more traditional. It can look sleekly upscale when used in a sophisticated herringbone pattern. A stone terrace or steps edged in used brick look more rustic. The warm tones of brick, its durability, its convenient size and shape, and its possibilities for patterning make it a classic garden flooring, whether as an accent or in large expanses. Because brick is more often used on houses than the other hard-surface garden materials, it can be very useful in extending architecture out into the garden; the same color and style of brick used on the house can be repeated in garden walls, paving, and trim.

WOOD. Wood has more advantages than can be easily summed up. It often echoes the material of the house and outbuildings; it can be stained or painted; it's durable and relatively inexpensive. Wood warms up metal, concrete, gravel, or any other material with which it is combined. It can look rustic and gnarled, or it can be stained smoothly

In the Netherlands, wooden platforms float on a lily pond, encouraging passage across the water.

gray for a modern look, left natural, or painted bright colors to fit into any garden scheme or style. Best of all, it can be changed as easily and inexpensively as slapping a new gallon of paint on a fence, chair, or arbor. Just be careful about where you use pressure-treated wood, for its chemicals leach into the soil and can be dangerous for food crops or pets. But pressure-treated wood can be used for the posts that go into the ground, and then wrapped in cedar to be stained or painted for a more versatile or livelier effect.

METAL. Metals are overlooked in gardens, which is too bad because they offer durability, strength, shine, and patina, and are lightweight besides. A sheet of galvanized metal can be used for a shed roof or framed in wood to form a gate. Hogwire makes a simple yet effective lattice on which to grow vines, or a screen that stops the eye yet lets light and air through. From copper caps, roofs, gutters, and containers to shiny steel screens or sculpture, metal has a surprising affinity to plants and the natural world, and looks its best paired with wood or other matte materials.

LIVING GROUNDCOVERS. Whether turfgrass, eco-lawn, or other kinds of plants that take some foot traffic, living groundcovers add interest and color while softening the garden. They give a place for kids and pets to play and roll around, invite you to spread out a blanket for a nap or a picnic, absorb sound, light, and rain. Because they usually stick up at least a few inches, groundcover plantings lend dimensionality to the garden. The Japanese tradition of planting mounds of overlapping groundcovers, or raised

beds only one board or brick high, emphasize this welcome characteristic of dimensionality near ground level, while allowing you to safely grow low plants that prefer not to be walked on.

Turfgrass is the most familiar and multipurpose of groundcovers, but it's a resource-heavy choice. Lawn needs mowing, edging, fertilizing, and watering to look its best, which wears out the gardener, spikes the water bill, and results in fertilizer runoff into streams and lakes. Although lawn used sparingly offers a soft, green open space, large expanses of flat lawn are often boring.

In recent years eco-lawn (also known as meadow-lawn, ecoturf, and environmental lawn) has become a more viable alternative as better regional seed mixes have become available. Not only does this looser, wilder lawn require less maintenance, water, and fertilizer, but it has

LEFT: *While lawn may squelch underfoot on wet days, this garden offers dry passage on stone and gravel softened with grasses and groundcover.*

RIGHT: *Recyclables never looked so urban-industrial-chic as in this garden, where wooden planters are backed by a metal fence built of drainpipes and gutters.*

A carpet of wooly thyme and a rare lion's mane maple turn what could have been a hard-edged stone terrace into a softer, more inviting space.

an appealingly tousled and casual look. A mix of various turf-type lawn grasses and drought-tolerant broadleaf perennials, eco-lawn takes a year or two to grow into a dense lawn-type planting. The mix of perennials and grasses varies around the country depending on soil and climate, so check with your local nurseries and agricultural extension service to find out which is best for your area. Usually the mix includes perennial ryegrass, clover for nitrogen, English daisies, and yarrow for a highly textural mix with spring bloom. It stays mostly green all year, with the lawn grasses green in spring and fall, and the perennials green during the summer when the grass goes dormant. These ecoturf mixes are very different from the wildflower mixes sold all too freely; while the latter sound like a good idea, many of them have proven to include invasive plants that choke out all the others in the mix, resulting in a ratty-looking meadow at best and a gardener's nightmare at worst.

A number of groundcovers are available that can take foot traffic, although few are as springy and comforting to walk on as lawn. Still, where they won't be stepped on too often, these groundcovers will soften the garden floor with color, texture, and bloom. The following can be planted between pavers, to grow out of gravel, or in expanses that once grown in will remain relatively weed-free:

- Ornamental strawberry (*Fragaria* 'Pink Panda' and *F. chiloensis*)
- Corsican mint (*Mentha requienii*)
- Barren strawberry (*Waldsteinia fragarioides*)
- Creeping thyme (*Thymus praecox*)
- Woolly yarrow (*Achillea tomentosa*)
- Carpet bugle (*Ajuga reptans*)
- Chamomile (*Chamaemelum nobile*)
- New Zealand brass buttons (*Cotula squalida*)

- *Euonymus fortunei*
- Small ornamental grasses and sedges such as the mondo grasses (*Ophiopogon* spp.), carexes (*Carex* spp.), and snow rush (*Luzula nivea*).

The stone pathway offers clear direction through mounds of plantings to a cushy oval of green lawn. A hazy scrim of Stipa gigantea *partly obscures the destination.*

RIGHT: *This mixed-media scene of meditative buddha with casual plant-ings, basket, and pots is saved from looking like a jumble by its framework of brick paving.*

BELOW: *Low stone walls add structure, texture, and dimension to this otherwise flat garden, as well as raise plants up for greater effect.*

FAR RIGHT: *The affinity of plants and natural materials like wood and stone shows clearly in the harmonious juxtaposition of spiky Japanese iris, smooth wooden bridge, and stone lantern.*

NEXT PAGE: *Plants are the most changeable of elements, and some are powerhouses of pattern-making. It's plants that make a garden vital, sensual, and emphasize seasonality.*

chapter ten

PLANTS

ICONIC PLANTS:

PATTERN-MAKING CHOICES

~ ~

PLANTS ARE ONLY A SMALL PART OF GARDEN pattern-making, even though they're what we usually think of first. It is plants that make a garden sensual and satisfying. It is their verdancy, growth, and seasonal change that transform gardens from outdoor rooms into places more intimate, compelling, and closer to our hearts.

A garden's dynamic and endless fascination comes from the green vitality that propels plants through their life cycle. We can't wait to step outside in the morning to see the parade of change through the seasons and through the years. Plants burgeon from the ground, leaf out, bloom, bear fruit, drop their leaves, wither and die, or surprise us by growing far larger than we are. Plants are ephemeral yet timeless in their predictable cycles, and it is this duality and metaphor that captures our imagination and beguiles us into becoming gardeners.

Whether through their shapes, fragrance, color, or blooms, certain plants are powerhouses of pattern-making. These plants seem to carry the distilled essence of "plantness" in their leaves and flowers, bringing more than their share of drama and excitement to the garden. It's true that a garden is made in large part from workhorse plants that cover the ground, form hedges, shield privacy. But it is the

Sunny yellow tulips backed by the fuzzy blue blooms of ceanothus are a quintessential springtime combination.

iconic plants offered in this chapter, arranged by what they contribute, that bring the gardener the most anticipation, satisfaction, and pleasure per square inch of garden space.

FRAGRANCE

Smell is the most primal and ancient of the senses, said to reside in our eons-old reptilian brain. A whiff of summer rain, lilacs, or sun-ripened raspberries can wrap us in nostalgia, flood us with a palpable ache of remembrance. Each of us has a plant or two we hold dear for their ability to so penetratingly and sensually evoke another time and place. While these memories are specific to our individual histories, certain scented plants seem to make so many people dreamy that they must tap into a deeper consciousness of fragrant memory. It's possible to plant scent throughout the seasons, from the headiness of roses and lilies to winter-blooming treasures that draw you out into the garden despite the chill. Seasonality can be celebrated not just with blossom and leaf change but with the fragrances specific to the time of year. These are the plants that carry the strongest, most beloved fragrances:

Winter

Witch hazels (*Hamamelis* spp.) are vase-shaped, deciduous shrubs to small trees that bear curious, spidery little flowers with a sharp, astringently sweet smell, pungent enough to scent a room when cut and brought inside. From December through March, witch hazels unfurl their flowers every day the temperature stays above freezing. The Chinese witch hazels, *Hamamelis mollis*, are the most heavily scented, with crosses such as *Hamamelis* x *intermedia* 'Pallida' also strongly fragrant. Most have bright yellow flowers;

Old-fashioned roses, like this delicate 'Ghislaine de Féligonde' remain the iconic summer flower. Their pastel frilliness and rich cold-cream scent bring back a collective memory of Grandma's garden, whether or not our grandparents ever put trowel to soil.

H. x *intermedia* 'Jelena' and 'Diane' flower in shades of copper and burgundy. Witch hazels are hardy, grow slowly, and turn shades of gold and orange in autumn.

Wintersweet (*Chimonanthus praecox*) is an ungainly, twiggy shrub with one of the juiciest of all winter fragrances. The waxy little pale yellow and purplish flowers smell deliciously fruity, sweet, and rich, coating bare branches in January and February. Plant at the back of the garden where it won't show in summer, but in winter you'll be searching the garden for the source of such penetrating perfume. Wintersweets are hardy, and flower most prolifically when planted against a sheltered fence or wall.

Azara microphylla is a graceful, small evergreen tree with tiny tufted flowers redolent of the tempting scents of chocolate and vanilla. Both glossy leaves and yellow flowers are at their best in February and March. The cultivar 'Variegata' grows more slowly than the species, with cream trim on each leaf. Azaras are slightly tender and hardy to zones 7, 8, or 9, depending on exposure.

Sweet box (*Sarcococca hookeriana* var. *humilis*) is a short (under 2 feet) evergreen shrub ideal for edging or groundcover, with shiny pointed leaves and tassel-like white flowers that bloom all winter. Their sweet vanilla scent is strong and persistent, even on the coldest days. *Sarcococca confusa* has equally desirable flowers and foliage, but grows into a larger shrub up to 5 feet tall. Sweet box is tough and hardy, prefers some shade from summer heat, and sports black berries after the flowers fade in springtime.

Mahonia x *media* 'Charity' is one of the tall Oregon grapes, growing 8 to 10 feet high. Its layers of jagged, gleaming evergreen foliage are topped off with sprays of fragrant yellow flowers, as beloved by bees and overwintering hummingbirds as by humans who crave such brilliant color and scent in January. *Mahonia japonica* is several feet shorter, is equally hardy and spiny, and has pale yellow wands of scented flowers.

February daphne (*Daphne mezereum*) blooms in the dead of winter, with rigidly upright branches coated in deep pink flowers as richly scented as expensive perfume. *Daphne mezereum* 'Alba' has snowy white flowers just as strongly fragrant; *D. bholua* 'Jacqueline Postill' also has fragrant winter flowers, but is hardy only to zone 8 or 9. If you add only one kind of fragrant plant to your garden, make it a daphne.

Viburnum x *bodnantense* 'Dawn' is a tall, somewhat gaunt shrub with handsome and ribbed leaves in summer. It shines from November through February, when it unfurls wave after wave of pale-pink, sweet-smelling flower clusters, seemingly impervious to whatever kind of winter weather rages around it.

Spring

Pheasant's eye narcissus (*Narcissus poeticus* var. *recurvus*) is a creamy daffodil with a cleanly outlined darker eye. Its surprisingly intense and spicy scent warms the garden on a chilly April morning; cut and brought indoors, a bunch can scent the entire house.

Hyacinths (*Hyacinthus* spp.) send up stiff stems covered in bell-shaped flowers with a pervasive rich fragrance, in shades from white to purple.

Lily of the valley (*Convallaria majalis*) has fresh-green pointed leaves that curl around sprays of little, dangling, white bell-shaped flowers with a fresh, clean fragrance.

Clematis armandii is a vigorous evergreen vine with leathery leaves and starlike creamy-white flowers in March and April that smell sweetly of vanilla.

Wisteria sinensis is a hefty vine with plumply drooping lilac-colored flower clusters so provocatively scented, especially on warm, rainy spring days, as to stir all the senses.

French lilacs (*Syringa vulgaris*), along with mock orange, must be the most immediately recognizable and eagerly awaited of springtime fragrances. Their cones of supremely fragrant blossoms, in shades from glistening white through deepest plum, come in single and double flowers, and are ideal for bouquets.

Sweet William (*Dianthus barbatus*) has pretty, clove-

scented flowers in late spring. Traditionally they have come in shades of pastels, but the 'Nigrescens' group has made this old-fashioned perennial newly popular, with their trendy dark stems and leaves topped with deep purple/brown flower clusters.

Osmanthus delavayi is a small-leafed, dark green shrub ideal for hedging. In March it is covered with tufts of sweet-smelling, clean, white trumpet-shaped little flowers.

Mock orange (*Philadelphus* spp.) is an old-fashioned shrub that redeems its ungainly shape with bright white, extremely fragrant flowers for a month in midspring to late

The delicate pale bells and fresh, clean scent make lily of the valley one of springtime's most necessary flowers.

*Witch hazels (*Hamamelis *spp.) are large shrubs bedecked with spidery, fragrant flowers in the dead of winter.*

spring. *Philadelphus* x *purpureomaculatus* 'Belle Etoile' has particularly pretty flowers with purple-blotched centers.

Korean spice viburnum (*Viburnum carlesii*) has large flowers (for a viburnum) with hot-pink buds opening to rosettes of white flowers that smell spicily of cloves.

Summer

Lavender (*Lavandula* spp.) has a pungent, herby smell that is classic midsummer. This gray-foliaged subshrub blooms with fragrant wands of flowers for many weeks, in shades from pale lavender to deepest, darkest purple. Spanish lavender (*Lavandula stoechas*) has two-toned flowers in an appealing rabbit-eared shape, but is more tender than most lavenders. *Lavandula* 'Munstead' is a classic, with deep blue-purple, very fragrant flowers on compact plants with gray-blue foliage.

Rosa 'Hansa' is a crinkled-leaf rugosa with deeply fragrant, ruffled, reddish purple bloom. Why would anyone ever give garden room to an unscented rose? Many of the hybrid teas lack fragrance, so beware. Old-fashioned English, Bourbon, and musk roses are especially fragrant, as are many of the rugosas.

Daphne odora 'Aureomarginata' has an all-pervading sweet perfume that announces spring as surely as the scent of sweet peas trumpets summer. This evergreen shrub has yellow-trimmed leaves and tiny pink flowers with nothing small about their scent.

Lilium 'Casablanca' is a quintessential Oriental lily: tall, stately, with huge showy white flowers so sweetly fragrant as to induce a swoon.

Honeysuckle (*Lonicera periclymenum*) is a vigorously

Like most lavenders, the fruity-smelling Lavandula angustiflora *'Jean Davis' is aromatic in both flowers and foliage.*

twining vine with highly scented tubular flower clusters, particularly fragrant in the evening.

Magnolia grandiflora has huge, glossy evergreen leaves garnished in summer with fat, creamy, cup-shaped blossoms smelling strongly of freshly cut lemon.

Sweet peas (*Lathyrus odoratus*) announce the beginning of summer with their penetratingly pleasing fragrance and ruffled blossoms in watercolor shades.

Heliotrope (*Heliotropium arborescens*) is an annual with dark crinkled foliage and clusters of tiny flowers in shades from lavender to dark purple, with an intense vanilla scent.

Mignonette (*Reseda odorata*), an assuming little annual considered to be the most fragrant plant in the world, is the stuff of French poetry. Its inconspicuous tiny pale flow-

ers hold their fragrance when cut and even after drying.

Nicotiana sylvestris is an annual flowering tobacco that grows into a candelabrum of green branches dripping scented white flowers. Because their sweetness is particularly pungent in the evenings, this is a perfect plant to grow beneath a bedroom window.

Common jasmine (*Jasminum officinale*), hardy only to zones 7 through 10, has shiny dark green leaves and starry little white flowers so sweetly scented as to evoke the tropics.

Autumn

Clematis rehderiana is a deciduous vine that blooms in early autumn, its leaflets dangling clusters of pale yellow bells smelling of fresh fruit.

Clerodendrum trichotomum is a small tree with sweetly scented white jasminelike flowers in autumn and heart-shaped leaves that smell like peanut butter.

Sweet pepper bush (*Clethra alnifolia*) is a large, rounded deciduous shrub with spicily scented white flower cones in early autumn, beloved by bees and butterflies.

Phlox maculata grows tall and blooms late, with pretty, open flowers in pastels that smell baby-powder sweet.

LONG-BLOOMING

Though a great joy of gardening is seasonal change, we also need plants that bloom dependably over many months. In spots of prime visibility or when your garden's color scheme depends upon them, long-bloomers are called for. Many are short lived, for they bloom their hearts out, which often shortens their life span to only a few years. But you'll find long-bloomers worth replacing,

Evening primrose is the "Energizer Bunny" of perennials, for it keeps on blooming month after summer month.

for nothing is as satisfying as a plant that flowers continuously through the seasons.

Wallflowers (*Erysimum cheiri*) have cheerful little fragrant flowers that begin blooming in March or April and carry on until frost. In shades from softest yellow through orange to lustrous mahogany, wallflowers, in their simplicity, can be either sophisticated or country-cottage.

Clematis 'Etoile Rose' has dark twining stems glossed with nodding rose-colored bells that open over several months from midsummer through autumn.

Lavatera 'Barnsley' is a quick-growing shrub with open, pale-pink, dark-eyed big blooms that continue to appear for literally the entire summer.

Daphne x *transatlantica* 'Summer Ice', a rounded evergreen shrub with white-trimmed leaves, bears pale, fragrant flowers for nine to ten months of the year.

Gaura lindheimeri is one of the longest-flowering perennials, with spikes of pink buds opening to starry white flowers.

Cape fuchsia (*Phygelius* spp.) is a slightly tender upright shrub with long, tubular flowers in a variety of shades that dangle off the bush for many months, attracting hummingbirds and bees.

Aster x *frikartii* 'Mönch' is the longest-flowering aster, with lavender-blue yellow-centered blooms that open from June 'til frost.

Solanum crispum 'Glasnevin' is a purple-flowered potato vine, slightly tender, that is covered in flowers all summer long.

Rosa 'Golden Showers' is a climber that opens redtinged buds to rich yellow flowers over many months. *Rosa* 'Iceberg' is another notably long-blooming rose, with white flowers.

Hydrangea serrata 'Preziosa' and *Hydrangea* 'Endless Summer' are deciduous shrubs with balls of beautiful flowers from June through frost. 'Endless Summer' is blue or pink, depending on the acidity of your soil, while 'Preziosa' starts out pink and mellows to shades of wine and purple.

Geranium endressii is one of the endlessly useful hardy geraniums that spread to cover the ground; its pink flowers bloom continuously from spring to autumn.

Evening primrose (*Oenothera fruticosa*) blooms during the day despite its name, and for most of the summer. It is a low-growing, floriferous perennial with cup-shaped blooms, in shades from yellow through orange, that open from purplish red buds on equally dark stems.

Escallonias (*Escallonia* spp.) are evergreen shrubs with small, shiny leaves and clusters of pretty little flowers in summer and fall. In milder climates, they may bloom for most of the year. Drought-tolerant and good for hedges and screens, escallonias are slightly tender.

Abelia x *grandiflora* 'Edward Goucher' is a twiggy, arching shrub that is semideciduous in most climates. It grows 3 to 5 feet tall and as wide, with small lilac-pink flowers over a very long season, starting in spring and carrying on through Christmas.

BIRDS, BEES, AND BUTTERFLIES

Creatures enrich our gardens as they live out their lives alongside our own. The tremor of a hummingbird's vibration or the flash of a butterfly's brief beauty allows us a glimpse of nature's mystery and rhythms. We can create a "safe zone," or network of gardens running through cities and suburbs to provide haven for birds, bees, and butterflies. If you create a healthy and hospitable environment by gardening organically with a wide variety of plants, the creatures will come. Not only plants but gardening practices are important: Eschew chemicals, plant mixed hedgerows for shelter and safety, provide fresh water, and don't be too tidy about cleaning up the spent plants that are a bird's favorite snack. Remember that wing beat, birdsong, and bee buzz are the hallmarks of a healthy garden.

Yarrow (*Achillea*), coneflowers (*Echinacea*), globe thistle (*Echinops*), sea holly (*Eryngium*), catmint (*Nepeta*), wall-

flowers (*Erysimum*), sedum, and rudbeckia are all perennials beloved by butterflies. If left to go to seed, they can also feed a wide variety of birds in the autumn. Skimmia, beautyberry (*Callicarpa*), snowberry (*Symphoricarpos*), viburnum, pyracantha, cotoneaster, elderberry (*Sambucus*), and other berried shrubs are important food sources for birds.

The most effective thing you can do to attract creatures to your garden is to add some native plants to the mix, for they have evolved over eons along with the local creatures in a web of mutual dependency. In addition to your own

*Wallflowers (*Erysimum *ssp.) are long-flowering, bee-and-butterfly magnets that come in a variety of cheerful colors, like this shrubby, melon-toned* E. linifolium *'Julian Orchard'.*

*Coneflowers (*Echinacea *ssp.) are as beloved by creatures as by humans, for they're handsome, long-blooming, and medicinal.*

regional native plants, here are a few other bird, bee, and butterfly magnets that are also wonderful landscape plants.

Hardy fuchsias are tough, late-blooming shrubs whose pretty, bright funnel-shaped flowers appear as if custom-made for a hummingbird beak.

Red flowering currant (*Ribes sanguineum*) is a Northwest native that first became popular in England. This large shrub with maple-shaped leaves bursts into a haze of deep-pink bloom in March, so it is an important early food source for hummingbirds as well as for butterfly larvae. A white cultivar is also available.

Bee balm (*Monarda*) is a tall, showy perennial beloved by bees and hummingbirds.

Roses with hips, such as the rugosas, which grow into a thicket rich with fall fruit, are favorite places for birds to congregate, shelter, and feed.

Wild lilacs (*Ceanothus* spp.) are slightly tender evergreen shrubs or groundcovers with blue blossoms in springtime. They're a source of food for butterfly larvae and adult butterflies, and bees love their sweet flowers.

Rosemary (*Rosmarinus officinalis*) has fragrant evergreen foliage, useful for cooking as well as for attracting hummingbirds and butterflies. (See also "Shrubs" in the "Minimal Care" section below.)

MINIMAL CARE

These plants have earned iconic status for their easygoing, dependable ways. Each obligingly clothes the garden

while pleasing the eye. Such workhorse plants free up the gardener to putter with fussier kin, or to focus on something besides the garden for a few minutes, and for this we are grateful. When correctly sited and watered in until well established, these plants require either no maintenance or one maintenance session a year.

Perennials

Autumn fern (*Dryopteris erythrosora*) is 2 feet tall, with russet-toned fronds that persist throughout the year. This fern needs only the old foliage trimmed back once the new fronds have emerged in springtime.

Wallflowers (*Erysimum*). See "Long-Blooming," above.

Sedum 'Autumn Joy' is just one of many kinds of sedum that are hardy, sturdy, and drought tolerant as well as long blooming. All they need is for the old foliage to be cut back in early spring as the new foliage emerges.

Donkey-tail spurge *(Euphorbia myrsinites)* is one of the easiest of this easy-care genus of plants. It is a prostrate grower, sprawling over walls or dripping down the sides of pots, with blue-green foliage contrasting with chartreuse spring blooms. You need only to give it a haircut in late autumn so the new foliage has space to grow in.

Mexican fleabane (*Erigeron karvinskianus*), a mounding perennial, is covered with tiny white daisylike flowers from March through December. Any exposure short of dank shade will do, and it is drought tolerant and blooms longer than any other perennial.

Lamb's ears (*Stachys byzantina*) are one of the most appealing groundcovers, with silver furry foliage and felted purple flower spikes. They prefer hot, dry sites but will grow anywhere, and need only to have the flower spikes cut off once they fade. Or grow the nonflowering version *S. byzantina* 'Silver Carpet' and you'll avoid even that one task.

Cotinus 'Grace' is easy-care like most smoke bushes, with especially large and shapely leaves that morph from wine-red through dark plum and hot orange-red.

Furry, silvery lamb's ears are one of the most tactile of plants that thrive just about anywhere you plant them.

Hardy geraniums are long-blooming groundcovers. From the wandering, yellow-leafed *Geranium* 'Ann Folkard' to the delicate, lacy *G. clarkei* 'Kashmir White', they have been called the "little black dress of the garden" for good reason.

Masterworts *(Astrantia* spp.) are long-blooming, sturdy, hardy perennials that do well nearly everywhere, with pretty buttons of flowers that last for weeks cut and brought indoors for arrangements. *Astrantia* 'Hadspen Blood' is deeply red; *A. major* comes in colors from white through pink.

Shrubs

Smoke bush (*Cotinus* spp.) offers a number of cultivars, with leaves that can be darkly purple, soft green, or glowingly golden. It needs nothing more than to be cut back late every winter to keep it bushy.

'Diablo' ninebark (*Physocarpus opulifolius* 'Diablo') is a dramatically dark-leafed shrub. The only thing difficult about it is pronouncing its botanical name; an occasional pruning back of its purple-bronze leaves to keep its size in bounds is all the care it needs.

Rosemary (*Rosmarinus officinalis*), although slightly tender (the lighter blue the flower, the hardier the plant), is evergreen to zone 7. These fragrant foliage plants are drought tolerant, and come in shapes from upright to trailing, so they can be used in garden situations from hedging to containers.

Mexican orange (*Choisya ternata*), an evergreen shrub with glossy leaves and fragrant white flowers, needs to be

Rosy flowered Sedum *'Autumn Joy' is a drought-tolerant late-bloomer, here mixed with asters and senecio.*

planted in a warm spot, for it's slightly tender (hardy to zones 7 to 9). *Choisya* 'Aztec Pearl' is more compact, with lacier foliage.

Beautyberry (*Callicarpa bodinieri* var. *giraldii* 'Profusion') is a hardy shrub so flashy in autumn and winter that you can't believe it's also easy care. Late in the year, the plant's upright branches are coated with little bright lavender berries so metallic and shiny they look spray-painted.

Sweet box (*Sarcococca* spp.). See "Winter" in the "Fragrance" section, page 187.

Abelia x *grandiflora*, a semi-evergreen shrub with fragrant little bell-shaped pink flowers that persist through summer, needs only a bit of thinning and cutting back when it gets too leggy.

Trees

Magnolia grandiflora 'Little Gem', a small evergreen magnolia, has copper felt on the back of every glossy leaf and white summer flowers. The only care this tree needs is occasional cleaning up of dropped leaves and blossoms.

Strawberry tree (*Arbutus unedo*), a small-scale tree with shiny green leaves and cinnamon-colored bark, is handsome year-round. It puts on a show in late autumn, when the round, warty fruits that earn it its common name turn red at the same time clusters of white flowers begin to bloom. Slightly tender.

Bulbs

Lilies (*Lilium* spp.) are little short of miraculous. How could plants so glorious and showy be easy-care? Find a spot with perfect drainage, stick the brown lump of a bulb into the ground in late autumn, and you'll feel like a wizard of a gardener in summer when you have a huge, fragrant lily like the snowy 'Casablanca' blooming atop a 6-foot stalk. All you need do is make sure the soil drains well and cut back the lily stalk after all the flowers fade, and you'll have a repeat show next year.

*Foxtail lilies (*Eremurus *ssp.) like this apricot 'Cleopatra' shoot up a tall and gaudy flower-coated spike from a rosette of leaves.*

Daffodils (*Narcissus* spp.), if planted in well-drained soil and left alone, will naturalize happily, returning yearly as a harbinger of springtime. Daffodil care is defined by what you don't do: Never cut them back, as the spent foliage needs to be left alone to wither away to feed the bulbs for next year. Daffodils prefer not to be watered in summer, and you don't need to worry about predation, because deer and squirrels don't fancy their bulbs.

FOCAL POINTS

Because of their architectural shapes, strong silhouettes, and flamboyant looks, some plants create garden focal points all by themselves. These are the punctuation points of the garden. Prickly or pointed, tall and skinny, or sump-

tuously large-leaved, the bold forms of such plants, and their sometimes startling presence, can save a garden from being merely pretty. Because they aggressively vie with each other for attention, though, too many showboat plants can create a feeling of unease and discord, with no place to rest the eye. But a few well-placed punctuation plants, from trees to groundcovers, can turn a blob of a garden into a dynamic and exciting space.

Mediterranean cypress (*Cupressus sempervirens* 'Stricta') is slender, elegant, and long-lived. It grows densely straight to 60 feet tall, forming a dignified exclamation point against the horizon.

'Skyrocket' juniper (*Juniperus scopulorum* 'Skyrocket') is a narrow column of a tree only 2 feet wide and 12 to 15 feet high. The foliage is bluish green, tight, and tidy, and the effect is of a crisp line drawing the eye up into the sky.

Flax (*Phormium* spp.) is a bold, bladed plant native to New Zealand. Some are more tender than others; the bronze *P. tenax* is the hardiest. Flax spreads into rigid, wide clumps that can reach 9 feet into the sky. Their dramatic vertical lines are emphasized in some cultivars by showy stripes, such as the olive and pink *P.* 'Sundowner', or the green, rose, and yellow *P.* 'Gold Sword'.

Crocosmia 'Lucifer' is a rock-hardy perennial with flowers so hotly colored you'd expect them to burn your hand if you touched them. This is an especially large crocosmia, with slender-bladed foliage nearly 5 feet tall and cascades of large, lipstick-red flowers from July into autumn.

Yuccas provide the ultimate vertical accent in the garden, with their stark silhouettes and tall spikes of creamy bell-shaped flowers. Their daggerlike leaves erupt from the soil in a variety of shapes, textures, and colors. From jagged edges to silvery blue blades, yuccas look more dangerous than pretty, although *Yucca gloriosa* 'Variegata' is softened by cream and hot-pink stripes. Don't write these off as simply desert plants, for they adapt to a wide variety of conditions. *Yucca baccata* is hardy down to 20 degrees below zero, and *Yucca gloriosa* revels in moist soil and humidity.

Alliums are showy onion relatives that look more like space ships hovering over the garden than bulbs that bloom dependably every May. *Allium* 'Globemaster' and *A.* 'Gladiator' both create a rhythm through the late spring garden, with 10-inch heads of starry dark violet flowers held high on 3-foot stems. *Allium giganteum* is the tallest at 5 feet. Star of Persia (*A. christophii*) is shorter, and its shimmery metallic-purple flowers are clustered into a bloom as large as a basketball.

Foxtail lilies (*Eremurus* spp.) grow from tuberous roots into imposing 9-foot-tall flower spikes. Plant in autumn for late-spring spires made up of masses of flowers in colors from pure white through shades of pink to bright orange.

Crown imperials (*Fritillaria imperialis*) look more like exotic parrots than plants. These lily relatives have stout 3-foot stalks dripping flower bells in shades of red, orange, or yellow, with a frilly topknot of glossy green leaves.

Carex morrowii 'Sparkler' is a dazzler of a groundcover, a green-and-white-striped grass that explodes from the ground more like a firecracker than a sparkler.

Euphorbia characias subsp. *wulfenii*, one of the largest and most exotic looking of the spurges, has tall, blue-green foliage topped with fat whorls of chartreuse flowers in earliest spring that look as if they should be growing undersea rather than in the garden.

Black mondo grass (*Ophiopogon planiscapus* 'Nigrescens') is perhaps the blackest of all plants. A spidery little grass with short blades in deepest, shiny ebony, it is frost-resistant and keeps its glossy good looks year-round.

LEFT: *The larger euphorbias are striking focal points even after their chartreuse flowers have faded. Here, the blue foliage of* E. characias *subsp.* wulfenii *plays against red barberry and fern fronds.*

RIGHT: *It's hard to believe that tall, slender, orb-topped alliums, like these elegant* A. giganteum, *are in the onion family.*

STRUCTURE

We tend to think of "structural" plants as the dependable, unchanging evergreens that form the bones of so many gardens in winter. Hedging plants and large trees provide permanent structure in the garden as surely as do arbors and fences, but gardeners shouldn't limit themselves to evergreens. During the seasons when we're outside the most, deciduous trees, perennials, and shrubs with presence form the living, changing architecture of the garden.

Gunnera manicata is a living sculpture of mammoth leaves, each stretching several feet across, that rise up out of the ground in an expanse of roughly textured thick foliage.

Hosta 'Sum and Substance' is a giant of a hosta and a glowing focal point. In a mature plant, which can form a huge clump 6 feet across, each ribbed, chartreuse leaf is 3 feet long.

Hosta sieboldiana 'Elegans' produces nearly as impressive a splay of ribbed foliage as 'Sum and Substance', but its leaves are a cool blue-green.

Yew (*Taxus baccata*), a classic conifer for hedging, is notable for its tightly woven yet soft texture, very dark green foliage, waxy red berries, and ease of pruning.

Wallich's wood fern (*Dryopteris wallichiana*) is a stately, vase-shaped fern with fronds reaching 5 feet high. New growth is dark and furry, unfurling to golden-green new fronds that age to rich dark green.

Mahonia x *media*, a majestic evergreen shrub that grows 15 feet high and nearly as wide, has jagged, glossy leaves that grow in layers up the stems. In late fall and winter, it sprouts spires of fragrant yellow flowers.

Golden catalpa (*Catalpa bignonioides* 'Aurea'), a large, hardy tree, can spread into a shady canopy if not cut back to the ground every year or so. It is grown for its huge, chartreuse heart-shaped leaves, which are at their biggest when the tree is cut back often enough so that it fits neatly into a border.

South African honey bush *(Melianthus major)* is a wonder, with floppy, serrated blue-green foliage that smells like peanut butter when you rub it. In a single season, these tropical-looking beauties grow 12 feet high and as wide, dying back to the ground in winter in colder climates.

Hosta *'Sum and Substance' has great presence in the garden with giant ribbed leaves in glowing chartreuse.*

An impressive display of structural foliage carries the garden through most months of the year, with layers of ornamental grasses, euphorbia, perennials, and bulbs.

Japanese maples (*Acer palmatum*) have such a graceful, spreading shape and such lovely bark that they bring presence and elegance to the garden in all seasons.

Cornus controversa 'Variegata' is a luxuriantly foliaged dogwood with a branching pattern so layered and horizontal that it's called the "wedding cake tree." In summer, the leaves shimmer with creamy white variegation; in winter, they fall to reveal the handsome branch structure.

MOVEMENT

Some plants give the feeling of motion and of wind even when the garden is at its most still. This illusion of waves, of wind, of rippling motion lends dynamism to a garden, creates a welcome beat of rhythm, and enlivens a garden no matter the weather.

Windmill palms (*Trachycarpus fortunei*) are the hardiest of the fan palms, keeping their exuberant foliage in temperatures down to 10°F. From its hairy trunk to its wide fans of foliage, this tree makes even the most temperate of gardens feel as if a tropical wind is always blowing through it.

Japanese forest grass (*Hakonechloa macra* 'Aureola', *H. macra* 'All Gold') is an easy-to-grow ornamental grass that appears more silky liquid than solid leaf. Whether striped in yellow, like 'Aureola', or a solid blazing puddle of gold, like 'All Gold', its slippery, shiny clumps appear to lap at the edges of a patio or pathway.

Mexican feather grass (*Nassella tenuissima*, formerly known as *Stipa tenuissima*), a little ornamental grass, is effective massed into waves of bleached-blond fluffs tossing their seed heads in the wind.

Farfugium japonicum 'Cristata' is a perennial whose big, round leaves are slightly fuzzy, with margins as scalloped as a piecrust. These pretty ruffled edges give the effect of the plant being buffeted about by wind or water even on the stillest day in the garden.

Bamboo, long revered in Asian gardens for the rustle of its clumps in even the slightest breeze, has a slim, tall silhouette and evergreen foliage ideal for screening. Do yourself a favor and choose a clumping type that doesn't run, such as *Fargesia nitida* or *F. robusta*, both of which grow into hardy, handsome clumps. Black bamboo *(Phyllostachys nigra)* is a runner that should be contained, but its striking glossy ebony canes make it well worth the trouble.

Heaths and heathers, when massed, have a liquid, undulating quality that often evokes the phrase "a sea of bloom." For year-round sweeps of color and texture, combine winter-blooming heaths such as *Erica* x *darleyensis* 'Ghost Hills' with summer-blooming Scotch heathers such as *Calluna vulgaris* 'Boskoop'.

Twisted Hollywood juniper (*Juniperus chinensis* 'Torulosa') looks as if it has weathered years of seaside gales. The needles twist and whirl around the trunk, as if perpetually swept up in their own little eddy of wind. These hardy evergreen trees grow 15 feet high.

Hinoki cypress (*Chamaecyparis obtusa* 'Gracilis') is a slender form of this popular evergreen tree that grows to 20 feet high, with whorls of foliage that appear to have

Ornamental grasses like this ruddy-toned Anemanthele lessoniana *seem to dance in the breeze even on windless days. The droopy blue blossoms of self-seeding* Cerinthe major purpurescens *continue the illusion.*

been blown about in high winds. 'Nana Gracilis' is a miniature form, and 'Nana Lutea' a dwarf version with bright golden foliage.

Blue weeping juniper (*Juniperus scopulorum* 'Tolleson's Blue Weeping'), with its combination of drooping branches and blue foliage, appears particularly drippy, bringing the sense of downward momentum to its every needle.

FLOWERING

Flower adoration is what starts most people down the slippery slope of gardening. Perhaps silky petals, vivid colors, and fluffs of stamens evolved to lure the bees, but we're just as attracted to them as the pollinators are. Even though flowers are fleeting compared to foliage, it is usu-

A garden scene is animated by lacy-leafed trees, perennials, and grasses that grow tall and willowy.

ally the scent, shape, and color of flowers that inspire plant lust. We all have flowers we can't imagine gardening without; here are a few of the essential ones.

Irises, from tiny, intricately patterned *Iris reticulata* to the water-loving Japanese iris and the over-the-top ruffles of bearded iris, are complex, charming flowers. Bearded irises come with frills, bicolors, and a fuzzy caterpillar-like stripe down each fall. Japanese irises are more simple and sophisticated, with open flowers and dramatic, swordlike foliage. Many irises are fragrant, all are gorgeous in a vase,

Red flowers heat up spring gardens. These lily-flowering tulips are among the most recognizable of flower shapes.

grow from tuberous roots into imposing plants with dozens of flowers. Dahlias with dark purple, bronze, and nearly black foliage, such as the intensely red-orange *Dahlia* 'Bishop of Llandaff' or the lilac-flowered *D.* 'Fascination', look fresh and most dramatic.

Long-stemmed hybrid tea roses may be the quintessential rose for the vase, but frilly, cold cream–scented old roses reign in the garden. From the crumpled, richly fragrant rugosas to fuzzy moss roses, queenly climbers, and elegant damasks, old roses remain the most beloved of all flowering plants. English roses, aka David Austin roses, such as the golden yellow *Rosa* 'David Austin' or the peachy-buff ruffle of *R.* 'Sharif Asma', are an inspired cross, with the scent and charm of old roses plus the long-blooming or repeat-blooming characteristics of modern roses.

Passion flower (*Passiflora* spp.), a slightly tender vine with characteristic corkscrew tendrils, produces one of the most intricate of all flowers. Faintly fragrant, in shades of greenish white, lavender, and purple, a single blossom is a work of art.

Clematis enchant with the variety and the loveliness of their blooms, from the nodding little bells of *Clematis alpina*, to the perfumed starlike blossoms of *C. armandii* and *C. montana*, to the showy, stamen-rich blossoms of the large-flowered species and hybrids.

Tulips (*Tulipa* spp.) must be, next to roses, the most instantly recognizable of flowers. Their fringed and blowsy glory inspired "tulip mania" in the Turks and the Dutch in the seventeenth century, when the price of a single prized bulb could bankrupt a man. Small, cupped species such as *Tulipa kaufmanniana* bloom in early spring. Lily-flowered tulips have spotted leaves and a profile as crisp and clean as a child's drawing, while the late-blooming doubles such as *T.* 'Angelique' are as seriously ruffled as an old rose.

Magnolias, with their waxy, lemon-scented flowers, are sumptuously exotic. Their curvy petals open to fluffs

and with careful planning you can have one type or another in bloom from winter through midsummer.

Dahlias might take for their motto "Everything old is new again," for these old-fashioned showboaters are newly trendy. And no wonder: they offer extravagant colors in a wild array of shapes from midsummer through frost. From tight little balls to dinner plate–sized wonders, dahlias of spidery stamens as long and thick as George Clooney's eyelashes. Furry buds open to flowers in purest white through clear yellow into shades of lavender and rose. Magnolia blossoms are extravagantly scented, and some, like those of *Magnolia* 'Star Wars', stretch nearly a foot across.

Pansies (*Viola* spp.) are perhaps the ultimate granny flower. The beguiling faces of pansies, violas, and violets make us feel nostalgic no matter whether our grandparents ever lifted a spade. Words like "nosegay" must have been invented for pansies and their diminutive relatives Johnny-jump-ups (*V. tricolor*), which look their best clustered together and close up, where their pretty little faces can best be admired.

Lilies (*Lilium* spp.)—stately, extravagant, and highly fragrant—grow from inauspicious lumps of bulbs into statuesque summer beauties. Asiatic hybrids, with speckled flowers that face upward, bloom early but are unscented. Orientals, martagons (*L. martagon*), and tiger lilies (*L. lancifolium*) all bloom midsummer to late summer, are supremely sweet scented, and come in various colors and shapes.

Wisterias (*Wisteria* spp.) are vigorous, twining vines with lacy foliage that drip long tendrils of white or violet-to-purple scented flowers in May. Graceful and flowing, a haze of wisteria in bloom looks more like a watercolor painting than actual flowers.

Poppies (*Papaver* spp.), from the hairy-budded, huge Oriental poppies (*Papaver orientale*) to the delicate Icelands (*P. nudicaule*) and the stunningly ruffled opium poppies (*P. somniferum*) that put Dorothy and her friends to blissful sleep in *The Wizard of Oz,* have showy stamens and tissue-thin petals in glorious colors from deep plum through all the sherbet shades.

Nasturtiums (*Tropaeolum majus*) are as easy to grow as they are quick to reseed. Open, spurred flowers in sunny colors from cream to maroon are familiar to every kid with a science project. Peppery scented, edible, and shown off

to perfection by their round, lily pad–like leaves, these are the ultimate cottage garden annual.

Sunflowers (*Helianthus annuus*) are cartoonlike in their appealingly exaggerated flower form. Rays of lemon-yellow, golden, or mahogany petals surround cushion-shaped disks of overlapping seeds beloved by birds. *Helianthus annuus* 'Mammoth Russian' grows 15 feet tall with flowers a foot across; *H. annuus* 'Teddy Bear' grows only a foot and a half high with double, pom-pom flowers.

Magnolia stellata unfolds silky, fragrant flowers in earliest spring, just when we most need encouragement that the garden will bloom again.

FOLIAGE

Flowers are fleeting, but foliage stays in place for many, if not most, months of the year. The longer you garden and the more sophisticated your eye becomes, the more you appreciate plants whose leaves are their main contribution. It used to be that garden colorists painted their effects with flowers; now there are enough variously colored and variegated foliage plants to create effective harmonies and contrasts solely with leaf color.

Rosa glauca is a rose you grow for its leaves, which are a striking pewter color, turning more coppery purple through the season. The rose is sturdy, hardy, and fountain shaped, with little pink flowers followed by bright red oval hips.

Leopard plant (*Farfugium japonicum* 'Aureo-maculatum') has big, round green leaves speckled with bright yellow spots. It reminds me more of a toad than a leopard. It prefers shade, where it grows to a showy 2 feet tall and as wide.

Canna are worth treating as annuals in cooler climates, and they take well to growing in pots set into ponds or in water-filled containers. Their huge paddle-shaped leaves come in shades of red and green, or even striped in purple, yellow, and pink, as in *Canna* 'Tropicana'.

*South African honey bush (*Melianthus major*) has handsome saw-toothed, blue-green leaves that children love for their dinosaur-like size and peanut butter fragrance.*

*Named a "Perennial Plant of the Year," Japanese painted fern (*Athyrium niponicum 'Pictum'*) is one of the loveliest small foliage plants.*

South African honey bush (*Melianthus major*) has lush saw-toothed foliage in a remarkable, shimmery shade of blue-gray-green. See description under "Structure," page 200.

Senecio greyi has the prettiest silver leaves of any shrub, and holds its foliage year-round. Each gray-green oval leaf looks as metallic as a coin, rimmed in silvery white, with a luminously white underside.

Heucheras may be the ultimate foliage plant, for their low-growing mounds of scalloped and ruffled leaves. These updated coral bells now come in shades from vivid chartreuse (*Heuchera* 'Lime Rickey') to semisweet (*H.* 'Chocolate Ruffles') and tones of apricot and spice (*H.* 'Marmalade'). Two new cultivars with the self-explanatory names of 'Mint Frost' and 'Peach Flambé' are stunners.

Smoke bushes (*Cotinus* spp.), while the hazy smoke-puff flowers are pretty, earn their place in the garden with their deep purple leaves (*Cotinus coggygria* 'Royal Purple'

or *C. coggygria* 'Velvet Cloak'). A newer cultivar with bright golden leaves that don't burn in the sun is *C. coggygria* 'Ancot'.

Acanthus mollis (bear's breech) is one of the most adaptable of plants, growing happily in wet shade or in near-desert conditions. Its huge clumps of glossy, deep green, lobed leaves stay fresh-looking most of the year, topped with tiered and layered flower spikes in summer.

Hostas, ferns, dwarf conifers, elderberries (*Sambucus* spp.), ornamental grasses, gunneras, banana trees, and most of the plants listed under "Focal Points," earlier in this chapter, are excellent foliage plants.

An old picnic table is greenly lush with foliage plants year-round; designed by George-Schenk.

WINTER INTEREST

No matter how inclement the climate, it's possible to have good reason to look out your windows year-round. From winter-blooming treasures to the most handsome "bones of the garden" specimens possible, these plants will coax you outdoors every month of the year while convincing you that gardens need never have an "off-season." In winter, we appreciate a garden's subtleties of shape and form, and we're led to notice its quieter beauties without the distraction of many flowers. See also the "Winter" section under "Fragrance," at the beginning of this chapter, for several additional suggestions.

Paperbark maple (*Acer griseum*) is attractive throughout the year, with pretty lobed leaves and vivid fall color. But in winter, when the leaves have fallen, revealing its cinnamon-colored bark, it becomes a focal point. The bark flakes and peels off in long, curling, papery strips so beguilingly that it's impossible not to finger it and pull it a bit to see the smooth, glossy trunk underneath.

Himalayan birch (*Betula utilis* var. *jacquemontii*) is a silvery white beacon in the winter landscape, growing 40 feet high, with airy leaves that turn golden in autumn. The pale tree trunks are dazzling when lit by low-slanting winter sunshine. Birches look their best grown in groves,

*Coral bark maple (*Acer palmatum *'Sango-kaku') is an essential winter landscape plant that's showiest after leaf drop when vivid pink-red twigs and bark are revealed.*

where their slender, ghostly shapes and color are magnified. European white birch (*Betula pendula*), paper birch (*B. papyrifera*), and Erman's birch (*B. ermanii*) are all white-barked birches of varying sizes and attributes.

Winter-blooming irises (*Iris unguicularis*) are hardy perennials that throw up short bursts of swordlike foliage and open their lavender-blue, white, or yellow flowers in the dead of winter. The flowers are honeysuckle-scented. *Iris unguicularis* 'Walter Butt' is pale violet and especially fragrant.

Tibetan or paperbark cherry (*Prunus serrula*) has rich red-mahogany bark so shiny it appears polished. Horizontal banding and peeling bark add to its winter interest. Because it tops out at 20 to 25 feet, it's an ideal tree for smaller gardens.

Redtwig dogwood (*Cornus sericea*) and yellowtwig dogwood (*Cornus sericea* 'Flaviramea') are twiggy shrubs that prefer damp soil and display dramatically colored stems in winter. Their color is most intense when these plants are cut back to the ground at least every other year. When massed together, shrubby dogwoods create colorful thickets of glowingly red or green-yellow stems.

Autumn-flowering or Higan cherry (*Prunus* x *subhirtella* 'Autumnalis') has a big flush of bloom in late autumn and then flowers sporadically through the winter. Even though the flowers are small and delicate, their semidouble fluffy paleness shows up well against a mostly brown or darkly evergreen winter garden.

Winter-flowering heaths (*Erica carnea* and *E.* x *darleyensis*) form durable sweeps of color through the winter. These needle-foliaged groundcovers flower from late autumn through springtime, in shades of white through purple. *Erica carnea* is the lower-growing of the two, while *E.* x *darleyensis* is bushier and grows 18 to 36 inches tall.

Erica carnea 'Foxhollow' has yellow foliage that turns a rich orange-red in cold weather; the familiar rosy pink *E. carnea* 'King George' flowers happily for months whether growing in a container or in a rockery.

Snowdrops (*Galanthus nivalis* and *G. elwesii*) are the quintessential flower that dependably pops up through the snow. Their delicate little white bell-shaped flowers, sometimes marked in green, nod among straplike blue-green leaves. These are the plants that will draw you outside on frosty mornings to see whether they've opened yet; some flower as early as Christmastime. *Galanthus elwesii* (giant snowdrop) is taller and sturdier than the common snowdrop (*G. nivalis*).

Cyclamen coum is another tiny winter beauty that is far hardier than it looks, with little winged rosy red, pink, or white flowers and showy, heart-shaped, ground-hugging leaves marbled in silver. Cyclamen spread into large colonies beneath trees and shrubs, and disappear completely in summer, to reemerge in November and bloom through February.

Christmas rose and Lenten rose (*Helleborus niger* and *H. orientalis*) are the showiest of winter flowers, with the Christmas rose often opening its snowy white blooms by late December. The lobed foliage is a rich green, and the flowers are charmingly simple, with overlapping petals in an open cup shape. The various hybrid hellebores are taller and sturdier and bloom toward the end of winter, with appealingly freckled flowers in shades from cream through yellow, pink, and darkest purple.

Evergreen hedging tends to disappear behind herbaceous plantings in summer but comes into its own after the leaves fall, when we rely on its green structure to carry the garden through the colder months of the year.

BIBLIOGRAPHY

The following books are ones I turn to over and over again for inspiration, information, visual stimulation, and sometimes comfort. I own hundreds of books about plants and gardens and I use many of them nearly every day; the ones below are the dog-eared favorites that form the core of my working collection.

I encourage gardeners to take full advantage of their public libraries as well as regional horticultural libraries, often associated with colleges and universities. Such resources offer a wide range of references and a worldwide selection of journals to keep us current while expanding our gardening vocabularies and sensibilities. Some of the books on the list are no longer in print, but you should be able to find them in libraries or from used book dealers.

Every bit as important to our development as gardeners is to look up from the dirt long enough to travel, visit art museums and galleries, tour public and private gardens, and appreciate all the arts. We train our eyes and exercise our creativities, learn more about color and design, by watching dance, reading novels, and paying attention to art, architecture, streetscapes, and fashion than by narrowing our field of study to plants and gardens.

Alexander, Christopher, Sara Ishikawa, and Murray Silverstein. *A Pattern Language: Towns, Buildings, Construction.* New York: Oxford University Press, 1977.

Brookes, John. *Small Garden: Ideas for Balconies, Terraces and Backyards.* New York: DK Publishing, 2006.

Chatto, Beth. *Beth Chatto's Gravel Garden: Drought-Resistant Planting Through the Year.* New York: Viking Studio, 2000.

Conran, Terence, and Dan Pearson. *The Essential Garden Book: Getting Back to Basics.* New York: Three Rivers Press, 1998.

Fell, Derek. *Encyclopedia of Garden Design and Structure: Ideas and Inspiration for Your Garden.* New York: Firefly Books, 2005.

Ferguson, Nicola. *Right Plant, Right Place: Over 1,400 Plants for Every Situation in the Garden.* New York: Fireside Books, 2005.

Hobbs, Thomas. *Shocking Beauty: Thomas Hobbs' Innovative Garden Vision.* Boston: Periplus Editions Ltd., 1999.

Hogan, Sean, ed. *Flora: A Gardener's Encyclopedia.* 2 vols. Portland, Oregon: Timber Press, 2003.

Juniper, Andrew. *Wabi Sabi: The Japanese Art of Imperman-ence.* Boston: Tuttle Publishing, 2003.

Martinelli, Janet, ed. *Plant: The Ultimate Visual Reference to the Plants and Flowers of the World.* New York: DK Publishing, 2005.

McVicar, Jekka. *Jekka's Complete Herb Book.* London: Kyle Books, 2005.

Pope, Nori, and Sandra Pope. *Color by Design: Planting the Contemporary Garden.* San Francisco: SOMA Books, 1998.

Schenk, George. *The Complete Shade Gardener.* Portland, Oregon: Timber Press, 1991.

Thomas, Graham Stuart. *The Garden Through the Year.* New York: Sagapress, 2002.

van Sweden, James. *Architecture in the Garden.* New York: Random House, 2002.

Wilkinson, Elizabeth, and Marjorie Henderson, eds. *The House of Boughs: A Sourcebook of Garden Designs, Structures, and Suppliers.* New York: Viking Penguin, 1985.

GARDEN CREDITS

Grateful thanks to all of the garden owners and designers represented by the photographs in this book and listed below. Note that if the garden was largely or completely designed by its owner, then no designer or landscape architect is included.

Pages 2, 26: Marocco garden, Richard Hartlage of AHBL design, Redding, CT

Pages 4, 42, 179: Dakin garden, Withey-Price design, Bainbridge Island, WA

Pages 6, 22, 34, 125, 126: MooseRidge Garden, Dominique Emerson design, Whidbey Island, WA

Page 10: Bruno garden, Steve Gold design, Seattle, WA

Pages 15, 150: Gulledge-White garden, Whidbey Island, WA

Pages 16, 70 , 95 , 101, 115: Juntenen garden, Mount Vernon, WA

Pages 18, 135 (top): Cannon garden, Seattle, WA

Pages 19, 96, 169: Doug Bayley garden, Seattle, WA

Pages 20, 106, 108, 129, 148: Tajima garden, Made Wijaya design, Palo Alto, CA

Page 25: Cavanah garden, Montesano, WA

Pages 27, 30, 43, 62, 92, 130: Terry Welch garden, Woodinville, WA

Pages 28, 73: Historic Val Verde garden, Lockwood DeForest design, Santa Barbara, CA

Pages 31, 53, 168, 171: Stacie Crooks garden, Shoreline, WA

Pages 32, 33 (bottom), 41, 63 (top, box), 93, 114, 146, 161 (top), 162: Easton garden, Lake Forest Park, WA

Pages 39, 48, 64, 71: Statler garden, Steve Martino design, Phoenix, AZ

Page 44: Private villa, Bali, Indonesia

Page 45: Van Dusen Botanical Garden, Vancouver, BC

Pages 46 (left), 133, 181: Portland Japanese Garden, Portland, OR

Page 46 (bottom): Harvey garden, Coupeville, WA

Pages 46 (right), 111, 127: Frederick garden, designed by owner with Rosemary Verey, Wilmington, DE

Pages 51, 65 (bottom), 124, 132, 145, 147, 178: Heg garden, Whidbey Island, WA

Pages 52, 74, 102 (middle), 112, 116, 119 (bottom), 120, 149: Vigil garden, Paul Repetowski design, Hansville, WA

Pages 54, 100: Stabbert garden, Bainbridge Island, WA

Pages 55, 59: Roberto Burle Marx garden, Rio De Janeiro, Brazil

Pages 56, 142: Nitzke-Marquis garden, Whidbey Island, WA

Pages 60, 134: Offenhauser garden, Pasadena, CA

Pages 61, 172: Colee garden, Robyn Atkinson design, Seattle, WA

Page 65 (top): Bob Chittock design, Vancouver, WA

Pages 66, 83 (bottom): Mark Henry garden, Snohomish, WA

Pages 68, 143, 144, 153: Miner garden, Anacortes, WA

Page 72: Feeney garden, Lake Whatcom, WA

Pages 75, 77: Portland International Gardens, Portland, OR

Page 78: Nitobe Memorial Garden, University of British Columbia, Vancouver, BC

Page 80: Portland Classical Chinese Garden, Portland, OR

Pages 81, 97: Scott Colombo design, Marin County, CA

Page 82 (top): Hulbert garden, Seattle, WA

Pages 82 (bottom), 117: Hirondelle garden, Port Townsend, WA

Pages 83 (top), 90, 102 (bottom), 110, 158, 167: Madoo, Robert Dash owner/designer, Long Island, NY

Pages 84, 87: Hummingbird Farm, Leslie Johnson and Ward Bebee design, Whidbey Island, WA

Page 88: Mico garden, Portland, OR

Page 89: Le Jardin de Rire Corbeaux (The Garden of the Laughing Crows), Richard Hartlage/Duane Dietz of AHBL design, Rocky Mount, NC

Page 91: Wagner-Waddoups garden, Portland, OR

Pages 93, 141: Virginia Hand garden, Seattle, WA

Pages 94, 119 (top), 156: Dorotik garden, Camano Island, WA

Page 99: Heronswood Nursery, Dan Hinkley and Robert Jones design, Kingston, WA

Pages 102 (top), 135 (bottom): LongHouse Reserve, Jack Lenor Larsen owner/designer, East Hampton, NY

Page 103: Chosin Pottery, Robin Hopper and Judi Dyelle design, Victoria, BC

Page 104: Elster garden, Virginia Hand design, Seattle, WA

Page 109: Ashton garden, Vancouver, BC

Page 113: Oyster Point Gardens, Nancy Heckler design, Poulsbo, WA

Page 118: Historic Casa del Herrero, Lockwood DeForest design, Santa Barbara, CA

Page 122: Ravenholt garden, Seattle, WA

Page 131: Raul de Souza Martins garden, Roberto Burle Marx design, Petropolis, Brazil

Page 136: Parnicky garden, Portland, OR

Pages 139, 177: Tilden garden, Portland, OR

Pages 152, 161 (bottom left): Jeff Bale garden, Portland, OR

Page 154: Knowles garden, Seattle, WA

Page 155: Clare Dohna garden, Vashon Island, WA

Page 157: Easton garden, Whidbey Island, WA

Page 159: Lee Kelly garden and sculpture, Oregon City, OR

Page 160: Thomas Allsopp garden, Seattle, WA

Page 161 (bottom right): Merryfield garden, Vancouver, BC

Pages 164, 174: Julie Moir Messervy design, Wellesley, MA

Pages 166, 176, 180 (bottom): Trinkle-Lane garden, Lisa Hummel design, Seattle, WA

Page 175: Moerheim Plantenwinkel, Mien Ruys design, the Netherlands

Page 180 (top): MacNab garden, Vancouver, BC

Page 182: MacDonald garden, Bothell, WA

INDEX